Contents

About the author

Patricia McBride is a management and interpersonal skills trainer. As well as running courses for people applying for jobs, she runs courses on selection interviewing so knows this topic from both sides.

Her interest in interview skills came about after performing very badly at an important interview. She was determined to learn how to do better and got the next job that she applied for. Using the guidelines she teaches in this book, the last time she went for a job interview, she had worked out every question that she was asked, with one exception.

Patricia's other publications include:

The EI Advantage, McGraw Hill, 2002

CVs and Applications, Lifetime Careers Publishing, 2004

Emotional Intelligence Activities Pack, Lifetime Careers Publishing, 2004

Acknowledgements

I would like to thank the following people for giving their time and assistance in writing this book: Doreen Dace, Rachel Dace, Helen Coffey, Patricia Duckworth, Julie Digby, Tina Bowen, Sam Lavender, Yasmin Croxford, Samantha Sherratt, Rick Leggatt, Avril Triggs, Vicky Shorland and Debbie Gregory.

Also, thanks to the Commission for Racial Equality, the DRC Helpline and the Equal Opportunities Commission for allowing me to reproduce material from their leaflets.

How to use this helpbook

This helpbook will be of use to you if you are aged between 16 and 21, although much of the information included would also help older readers. It will help you whether you are being interviewed for a job or for a place at college or university.

Although there are differences between the two types of interview, there are many similarities. This helpbook will give you all you need to know to prepare ahead and shine on the day. You will find case studies, quotes, examples and checklists to make you think long and hard about how you approach the interview situation. Also, it will give you lots of information and improve your confidence in your ability to perform.

How this book is organised

Each chapter begins with a brief summary of what is covered and at what stage of the interview process you should read the chapter. If you spend a few minutes reading through these before you read anything else, you will be able to use your time effectively. There is also a checklist at the end of each chapter that acts as a useful revision aid or quick reference.

It is unlikely that you will need or want to read the book in one go, although it would certainly be helpful if you could do so. The point is to use the book in a way that is most helpful to you.

You can learn a lot from reading how to do something, but even more from actually doing it. For this reason, there are a number of activities in the book. These activities are designed to get you thinking effectively about yourself in relation to the interview process. Time spent completing them will be time well spent. But please don't feel that you have to do every activity. Choose those activities which cover the areas where you need to improve your skills or self-awareness.

Your interview file

To help you make the most of this book and your chances at interview, I suggest that you get yourself a file of some sort (ring binder or envelope). You will need to keep in the file:

- details of each job or course that you apply for

- copies of application forms or CVs that you've sent out (remember to take copies of them – it will save time when filling in the next one and help your interview preparation)

- your answers to the activities in this book

- your record of how well you did in your mock interview

- your review sheets to follow each interview.

But before we look in detail at interview techniques, here are the experiences of two people who have already been through the interview process. Their stories will highlight the great variety of ways in which interviews are conducted.

Tina's story

'I went for an interview for my first job when I was still at school. The job was working for a district council. I would be work-shadowing and would get day-release to do a course on one day a week over a year, which was the equivalent to a two-year full-time course in college, and of course I'd get paid. Other than that, I didn't know much about the job or the place before I went and so I didn't really know if I even wanted it.

The college said my mum had to take me to the interview and I was really glad, because I felt more confident with her there. Even so, I was really nervous. I was expecting the interview to be really formal and strict, like school. Our school hadn't given us much idea of what to expect.

I had a letter telling me where to go, and that bit was all straightforward. When one of the interviewers came to get me, she was enormous, absolutely huge – I felt completely overpowered. She took me into a tiny interview room and the other interviewer was nearly as big! They seemed to fill the room. They sat some distance away from each other so that it was difficult to keep them both in view at the same time. We sat in low comfortable chairs in a triangle, with me nearest the door. Ready to make an escape if necessary!

Still, I needn't have been so nervous; they quickly made me feel relaxed. In fact, they were much more human and understanding than the interviewer who I saw for a place at college.

They seemed to do most of the talking. They told me all about the district council and that I would be able to try working in different departments. I was really excited about this, especially when they said I could try working in Personnel — something I really wanted to do.

I can't remember many of the questions they asked me – I don't think they asked many. I do remember though that they asked me what I wanted to do in the future and how I thought I'd do in my exams. They told me I'd only be offered the place if my exam results were okay.

For part of the interview, one of them went outside and spoke to my mum whilst the other chatted to me. I don't know what she asked my mum.

That was it really. They shook my hand and showed me out. I left determined to work even harder at my exams so that I could go to work there.

I got the place and loved the job, especially working with the large lady who turned out to be really good fun!'

Sam's story

'I recently had an interview for a place on an English and American literature degree course in a university in the Midlands.

Our sixth-form college is pretty good about interviews and one of the teachers gave me a mock interview the day before. He told me he would be really mean during the interview and he was. It was very good practice (and the interview wasn't nearly so bad).

I travelled to the Midlands by coach and got off at the wrong town! I had to quickly get a train the rest of the way. Luckily, I had allowed plenty of time and still got there okay.

Before the interview, prospective students were shown round the whole college in groups of four, each group being escorted by two first-year students. It was good, we got a chance to know each other and chat as we walked round. The college was very impressive. I liked it. After the tour, we were given a cup of tea in the common room while we waited for our interview. We were all a bit nervous and, as we were all applying for the same course, we kept asking each other the sort of questions we thought the interviewer might ask.

A lecturer from the course interviewed me. She took me into her office, and we sat on a couple of comfortable chairs. The desk was against the wall, not between us. I think I had been expecting two hard chairs and a bright light shining in my face! She was very friendly and informal. She asked me first about my journey, and I told her the problems I'd had. A stroke of luck was that she used to teach at my school some time ago, and knew one of the teachers quite well. We spent about ten minutes talking about that.

After the more informal bit, she began to ask me about my A levels. As I said, I had been very worried I wouldn't be able to answer some questions, so I had done a lot of preparation. I had spent time noting ten points I wanted to get across and also thought about how I could make links between the A level subjects I had chosen as well as between the different books I had been reading for English A level. I was determined to have some say in the way the interview went. Also, I was worried that I might get asked questions on American literature and I wanted to avoid that because I haven't read any.

Actually, I needn't have worried. I was expecting a succession of questions thrown at me so rapidly that I wouldn't have time to think, but there was plenty of time to talk about each question, and none were really tough. We talked about English literature and I managed to keep quite a lot of control of the interview by thinking ahead to what questions she might ask about what I was saying. This meant I could say things like "Well, you might think" and go on to give a reasoned argument for what I was saying. Not that she made it difficult. She encouraged me to keep speaking by nodding and saying things like "And what else do you think?" In fact, a couple of times the conversation seemed so easy that I wondered if I was being overbearing because I was doing all the talking, so I stopped and said, "What do you think?"

We also talked about high and popular culture, including a couple of programmes on television at the moment. Fortunately I'd seen them both. One is an adaptation of a book we're reading for A level and we discussed different aspects of that. Really, I could forget it was an interview. It seemed like chatting to a friend about a subject we were both interested in.

At the end of the interview, she asked me if I had any questions. I had a couple prepared ahead of time and asked her those.

I don't know if I'll be offered a place, but she was speaking as if I would. I really enjoyed the interview and feel much more self-confident now that I've been through one.

My advice to anyone facing an interview would be to decide what points you want to make and to think of all the objections the interviewer can make. That way you can pre-empt them. Make sure you get the chance to talk about the things you want to cover, but admit if you don't know something. Your mind shouldn't ever go blank if you've done enough preparation.'

Chapter one
Types of interviews

You should read this chapter:

- preferably no later than one week before the interview.

By the end of this chapter you should know:

- the range of different interview types that you may face

- why interviewers use different types of interview.

Into the torture chamber

Interviews can be scary or fun, depending on your attitude – some people see them as a great chance to find out about a job and to talk about themselves non-stop. The great thing is that by preparing yourself, you can really enjoy your interview. Throughout this book we'll look at ways to prepare yourself, but first, let's look at the types of interview that you may face.

Remember that an interview is a two way process – an opportunity for the interviewer to find out about you and for you to find out more about the college or job you are applying for. Approaching an interview from this perspective gives a much more balanced view and gives you back a sense of control. Having said that, you need to be aware that there are interviews and interviews. If you haven't been told what type of interview you will be facing when you arrive, don't hesitate to phone first to ask – it's okay to do so, and you owe it to yourself to be as well informed as possible.

Don't be surprised if they can't say exactly how many people are interviewing you. It's not unusual for these things to be left to the last minute. While some organisations are superbly professional and organised about interviews, others are amazingly unstructured. You may be surprised to know too that many interviewers are quite frightened before interviewing people. It's not something that most employers do often, so sometimes they feel quite unskilled and unsure.

One-to-one interviews

As the name suggests, a one-to-one interview is when you face just one interviewer working alone. This is often the case when you apply for a relatively low level job, and for some college or university courses.

This is probably the least stressful type of interview (from your point of view), as you only have to relate to one person. The disadvantage is that there is only one person's view of you, and if that's wrong there is no one else to challenge it.

Occasionally, you may be faced with a series of one-to-one interviews. Colleges, universities or organisations may do this when, for example, you would be working or studying in several different areas, or when different people are needed to explain different aspects of the job or course.

Typical interview format for one-to-one, or one-to-two or three interviews is:

Welcome, introductions (to the panel)
Interviewer tells you the format of the interview
Interviewer gives you additional information about the job
Interviewer asks you questions
You have an opportunity to ask interviewer questions
Interview ends

One-to-two or three interviews

This is a very common format, both for jobs and college or university interviews. It is slightly more difficult for you to relate to more than one person, but two or three is not too bad.

Probably your most difficult task is deciding who to look at. There's a simple rule. Look mostly at the person who asked you the question, but shift your gaze from time-to-time to take in the other person or people. You probably do this without thinking when talking to friends, but self-consciousness in an interview sometimes robs us of our natural body language. Next time you're with two or three friends, practise until you can comfortably handle appropriate eye contact.

The advantage of this type of interview is that there are several opinions of you which will give a more measured view.

Panel interviews

It is unlikely that you will be facing a panel interview at this stage in your career, but it is worth being aware of them just in case.

In a panel interview you will be facing a whole heap of people. Interviewers may use this style when they want to share the decision for some reason. Alternatively, they may wish to appoint someone who will work with all of them, and therefore they all want to have a say in the final choice that is made.

If you are faced with more than three people, it can be difficult to keep them all within your gaze at the same time. This is especially true as the more of them that there are, the further away you are likely to be seated, because they all need to be able to see you too. As before, the trick is to give most attention to the person asking the question. However, you must look occasionally at the other interviewers. If there are too many people to look at individually, you can look at them in 'groups' of three or four. Try it at a party some time, it does work.

Group interviews

This can take any one of a number of forms. Group interviews are used sometimes in addition to a one-to-one or one-to-two interview.

In this scenario, the group is not the candidates (although they may be together), but a group already existing at the university, college or workplace. The purpose of this type of interview is to give the team of people that the successful candidate will work with an opportunity to meet them and pass on their thoughts. It also gives you an opportunity to ask questions in a more informal setting. Occasionally, it is for observers to check out your group behaviour. Here are some variations on this theme:

Meet the team members

In this type of group interview, candidates are placed in different rooms, alone, and existing members of staff will wander from room to room, chatting to each of the candidates. This can be a fairly relaxed and informal feeling procedure. Don't be fooled – unless you are told otherwise, assume that it's part of the formal process – it usually is.

> *'Some of the candidates seemed completely thrown at having to join in a group discussion. They slumped in their chairs and this gave a very poor impression.'*

Quote from a manager interviewing candidates for a senior post

Group task

Occasionally, you may be asked to work with other candidates to solve a problem. This is not unusual in interviews for officership in the Armed Forces or for some management jobs. The task is likely to be something which should show the observers how you behave as a team member, how innovative you are, whether you display leadership qualities and how well you think on your feet.

If you know that you are going for this type of interview, it is unlikely that you will be told what the task is in advance, and this makes preparation difficult. However, you might consider looking at a book on leadership skills or trying to talk to other people who do similar work to see what pointers you can get.

Group discussion

This method can be used in both job and college or university interviews.

All the candidates are seated together (usually round a table) and are given a topic or case study to discuss.

The purpose of the discussion is for the observers to learn more about you. It is worth keeping in mind that negative qualities displayed by people in groups are aggression, rudeness, domination, stubbornness, criticism of others and prejudice.

Positive qualities include summarising what has been said so far, sharing ideas, showing consideration for others, making regular contributions to the discussion, keeping to the topic, flexibility, good body language and good listening skills. Showing a sense of humour is also great, but don't overdo it.

For example, if you are applying for a job which involves negotiating or lots of meetings, you may well be given a topic to discuss which should demonstrate your skills in these areas.

Obviously, discussion topics will vary according to the organisation and the job, university or college place that you are applying for, but may be along the following lines.

- Discuss where this organisation (or service) will be in five years time.

- Discuss the role that this organisation can play in the future of ...

- What do you think the main problems facing ... are today?

- How could ... be improved?

If, however, you are applying for a place on say, a social work course, it is more likely that the observers will be checking out your attitudes. For example, you may be asked to discuss the priorities which should be given to distributing a limited budget to various needy groups (some at least will be potentially controversial), or the best way to help a particular client group.

There are endless variations on the group interview, these are just some suggestions so that you can get a feel for what to expect. Don't forget that you can ask for at least a rough idea of what is likely to be involved in the whole interview process before the big day.

Annabelle's story

'When I finished college I had an interview to join the Air Force. It was a weekend-long interview and covered just about all the different types of interview you could imagine. It started with a basic IQ test, some written and some looking at pictures – that bit was quite stressful, but not too bad. After that there was a very extensive medical examination to see if we were fit enough. Then we had group activities — they were really fun. We had to do things like roll a barrel across a plank without it falling off. Some of these exercises were done to highlight group cooperation, but then we each had to lead a group on a task. Then we were back in the classroom and had to work in groups of about six to solve a written problem.

Up until then I had been having a great time. The other people applying were interesting and we all enjoyed it. After I got home though I realised that I had really messed up the last bit. That was an observed group discussion. We were given a list of topics to discuss – I remember two were "Fox hunting should be banned" and "Cannabis should be legalised". It didn't even occur to me to think what would be considered the official line on any of the topics, I just said what I thought. Looking back, I was so naïve that I can hardly believe it – I should have said what they wanted to hear. I didn't get accepted.'

Internal interviews

This can happen if you are going for another job where you already work. If you are a student it might be the case that you are trying to change your course part-way through, or applying to take a higher qualification in your existing college or university.

One problem with internal interviews is that you can fail to take them seriously. This may because you know the set-up inside-out, share your coffee breaks with the interviewer, feel embarrassed because they know you (warts and all) or simply feel over confident. **Don't**. Treat this interview as seriously as any other. Don't slouch, make in-jokes or moan about difficult people that you both know. Remember: if there is competition for the job or place, the other candidates will be trying hard to put on a polished performance – can you afford to do less?

A second problem is that the people will know you too well, and their ideas about you may not be accurate. It may be that you will have to work hard to overcome some prejudices on their part, if any exist. Again, treat the interview as seriously as any other, considering all the points you need to raise to sell yourself effectively.

Informal interviews

You may just be asked to attend a lunch or go to a pub with the existing work team or students, so that they can meet you. This may be a truly informal meeting, with no feedback to the formal interviewers, or actually it may be part of the formal process in disguise. Eitherway, just be yourself, use your preparation and **don't drink alcohol** no matter how tempted you may be. You may say something that you later regret.

Advertised interviews

Sometimes you will see companies advertising that they will be interviewing people for jobs at a certain place on a certain day. These often seem to be sales jobs and frequently the interviews are held in hotels. You may not be expected to ring for an interview (but check the wording of the advertisement). You simply turn up on the day and wait to be seen.

Different companies run these differently. Some will do a formal interview on that day, while others will simply tell you about the job, and give you a form to take the application further if you are interested.

Telephone screening interviews

To save time, some employers or agencies conduct a preliminary screening of candidates by phone. Your preparation in completing your application form or CV will pay off here. You should be clear about the skills that you can offer and why you want the job.

In-person screening interview

In some organisations human resource managers do an initial screening of candidates face-to-face. This is to establish a preliminary impression of your attitude, interest and professional style. Prepare for this as thoroughly as you would for the 'big' interview. This type of interview is carried out by employment agencies also on behalf of organisations looking for staff.

Work sample interview

Sometimes you may be asked to present your skills at interview. Perhaps you will be asked to do a presentation, or show a portfolio of your work. Typists may be asked to type a letter and administrators may be asked to compose a letter. See Chapter seven – *Tests for selection* for more details on this.

Video conference interview

Some companies use video conferencing to hold meetings or conduct other aspects of their business. Conducting an interview this way saves a lot of travel time and costs and is effectively a face-to-face interview. If you're nervous about sitting before a camera, practise beforehand. You'll be surprised how quickly you forget that it's there.

Hidden interviews

Some employers might send you off on a tour of the office, factory or whatever with an underling. You chat away innocently, saying how terrified you are at interviews, how you don't really have the skills they're after, or, worse still, you treat the underling with less respect than he or she deserves. And what happens? Prior to your formal interview they feed all this back to the interviewer!

So, if you're asked to take part in anything of this nature, be friendly, polite and interested. Do not disclose weaknesses. This is equally true of the time that you spend sitting in the reception office – you may be being watched. You have been warned.

Assessment centre interviews

The term 'assessment centre' is misleading because it is a process rather than a place. Some organisations now realise that interviews are not in fact a good way of predicting future success in their chosen candidate. For this reason they ask candidates to attend an assessment centre, where the candidate is given a range of different tests to assess their skills and personality. This is found to be a much more accurate way of judging future success.

Usually several candidates attend an assessment centre together. They will undertake a range of tests, some individually and some as a whole group. The formal interview may be undertaken also at this time. Assessment centre interviews can last as long as two days.

If you are asked to attend an assessment centre, congratulate yourself. These are expensive for employers and they do not invite candidates to attend unless they are serious about them.

While assessment centre activities vary, certainly there will be people there to guide you through the process. Also, there will be observers and assessors to note your performance. If you have any disabilities that make any activity difficult, discuss it with the employer beforehand.

You would be well advised to check whether your Connexions/careers centre has any information on assessment centres. They may be able to give you practice sessions.

At an assessment centre you may find yourself involved in any of the following:

- an informal event where you get a chance to meet other candidates, the selectors and managers from the organisation. This is a good opportunity for you to really find out about the organisation

- information-giving sessions – do listen carefully. You may be expected at some stage to show that you have digested all the material and can talk about it

- activities – (many of which are discussed in the remainder of this chapter)

- formal interviews.

Preparing for an assessment centre

Study the organisation

Before attending an assessment centre, prepare thoroughly. This is very important. Investigate as much as you can about the organisation – its past, present and planned future, its 'style' (caring, thrusting, etc.). Also, look at current issues in the field in which the organisation operates – social, technological, ecological and political.

Commonly-used exercises

Interview simulations/role plays – in this activity you will be expected to discuss a topic with a 'resource person' and to try to reach agreement on a disputed issue. You are often given 15-30 minutes' preparation time. While you are scored generally on your discussion, sometimes your notes are taken into account. It is sensible therefore to make your notes clearly and define distinct goals for your conversation.

In-tray exercises – this is generally an individual activity. You will be given a pile of correspondence and be expected to deal with it. It will be assumed that you are new in the post and have 'inherited' the correspondence. Your only indications of what to do with the correspondence are in its content, plus any annotations that have been made on it beforehand. When deciding what to do with each item, make sure that you mark everything clearly so that the assessor knows what action you would take. The assessors will be looking for evidence that you have a logical way of prioritising work (look in time management books for advice on this if you are not sure).

Group discussions – in this type of exercise you are likely to be part of a group discussing a particular topic. It may be that you are asked to form a committee to decide how to spend a budget, be part of a meeting making decisions for the future of an organisation or any other discussion appropriate for the post in question.

Groupwork – you and other candidates could be put together in a situation and you must decide between you how to resolve it. The situations could be relevant to business, for example, a scenario where your shop is failing and you have to find a way to make sure that you sell all your goods before Christmas. Alternatively, you could be faced with a theoretical exercise. For example, your group is lost at sea and you only have ten specified items to help you to safety. You have to decide which items are most important. The aim of this type of exercise is to see how you behave in a group – who takes leadership, how well you communicate, how cooperatively you work, and so on.

Outdoor activities – For example, you could be expected to find treasure using the clues provided. You could be just left at an unknown destination and have to find your way back. You could be taught to absail. If you have any disabilities which would make this difficult, discuss this with your potential employer or the university or college beforehand.

Case studies/analysis activities – this is generally something that is undertaken individually. You will be asked to write a report or brief on a given topic and will be provided with information to do so. Make sure that your report or brief is well written and that you have reached a decision about the topic under consideration. Although graduates are bright people, some have poor skills in writing. If this is true for you, find a way to polish your skills beforehand.

Presentations – you may be asked to give a presentation of some sort – this is particularly true for technical people. You could be presenting information on behalf of the group that you are working with, or you could be presenting information on a topic you select or that is given to you.

Psychometric tests

These tests assess aspects of your personality. You can read more about them in Chapter seven – *Tests for selection.*

Vicky's story

'I went to an assessment centre for a place as a graduate trainee with a local authority. It was a packed day. We did a psychometric test, had tests of numeracy and verbal reasoning. We also had to write a report based on a case study they gave us and finally a group discussion. Only the people who got through that lot got invited back for formal interviews.

My advice would be to do as much homework as you can and then just enjoy the day. I certainly did and even made two new friends from the others doing the same tests. Oh, make sure you get a good night's sleep beforehand! I'm pleased to say I got the place and four years later still work with the same local authority in a management position.'

Chapter checklist

Have you:

- found out about the nature of the interview?

- practised skills, if they are likely to be tested?

- investigated how long the interview will be?

- checked out how many interviewers there will be?

- practised speaking to two or more people using appropriate eye contact?

- kept up-to-date with current issues in your chosen subject/work?

- thought about what attitudes interviewers or group observers may be expecting to see?

- considered your views on issues relevant to the course/job so that you have something to discuss?

- identified your own group behaviour in this type of situation, to decide whether it is positive or not?

- noted examples of relevant experience to discuss at any stage of the interview?

- considered how your educational qualifications will help in your application?

Chapter two
How interviewers score you, and other interview rules

You should read this chapter:

- about a week before the interview.

By the end of this chapter you should know:

- how interviewers score candidates at interview

- the 'rules' of interviews for candidates

- the 'rules' of interviews for interviewers

- the mistakes that interviewers might make and how to overcome them

- how to make a good initial impression

- how to provide information if you are not asked the right questions

- how to cope with unfamiliar jargon and abbreviations

- how to deal with silence.

Think like an interviewer

Trained interviewers behave in a fairly predictable way and this makes your interview preparation much easier. Chapter five *Sample questions and stunning answers* tells you how to anticipate the questions that the interviewer might ask you. In this chapter we'll concentrate on how interviewers score your answers and some general rules of the interview game. For information on how to anticipate the questions that you might be asked, read Chapter five.

How interviewers score

Trained interviewers will score you at interview against the questions that they have devised and against any tests that they have given you. (Some interviewers are not trained and do unpredictable things, but the problem is that we can't predict this!) Let's look at a typical interview score sheet, in this case for a clerk/typist post. You will see that the interviewer has written the questions on the left, and has left a space for comments and a score on the right. Typically, interviewers will be grading you numerically, perhaps on a one to ten scale.

Question	Comments	Score
'Why do you want this job?'		
'What skills do you think you can offer us?'		
'This is a busy job. How would you prioritise your work?'		
'What features of Word can you use?'		
'What is your typing speed?'		
'Give me an example of a time when you worked using your own initiative.'		
'Give me an example of a time when you worked as part of a team.'		

They should make (polite) comments about your answers, especially as you are allowed to ask to see their score sheets.

Interviewers will complete the forms and give the job to the person who scores the highest. If there is more than one interviewer, this and other scoring systems can ensure that judgements are made objectively. This should help to avoid a situation where one interviewer sways another in their opinion.

Many organisations base their scoring systems on the items in the job description and person specification. Many will concentrate only on the items in the person specification – sometimes called 'competencies'. Later in this book you will learn more detail on the difference between a job description and a person specification, but briefly, a job description describes the job to be done (the tasks), while a person specification describes the person who can do the job (their competencies).

When you have worked through Chapter six on questions and answers you can practise interview questions with a friend and ask them to score you using this type of system.

Rules for candidates

Interviewing is a game and you have to play by the rules. However, it is true that many people, even those with wide experience, age and qualifications do not always follow these rules, and failure to do so can mean you lose the game. Here are some of the rules – follow them and you'll be streets ahead of the competition.

1. Be punctual.

Better to sit outside for half an hour waiting for your appointment than to make a bad impression before you start. Ideally, aim to arrive 15 minutes before your interview time.

2. Be polite.

Never, ever be rude to *anyone* throughout the whole application and interview process. This is true even if someone does something so horrendous that you wouldn't touch the place with a bargepole. The world is a small place and you never know where people will turn up next. If someone does something unforgivable, such as making a racist comment and you feel you must do something about it, comment assertively and take up the matter with the dean of the college or university or the managing director after the interview. (You may choose also to get in touch with relevant organisations – see the Chapter eight *Equal opportunities issues* for more details.)

3. Never eat during an interview.

If you're gasping and you're offered a drink – go for it, being nervous can make your mouth go dry. But it's really difficult to give convincing answers while you're munching a biscuit.

4. Never smoke during an interview.

You need to be able to use your hands naturally to convey feelings. If the interviewer is a non-smoker you may be instantly crossed off their list.

5. Use appropriate body language.

More on this in Chapter four.

6. Never complain about anyone.

So your English teacher was useless and that's why you got a bad result, or you had to leave your job because you couldn't stand the idiot at the next desk. Don't say so. The interviewer won't be able to tell if you're telling the truth or if there's something wrong with you. Interviewers want people who will take responsibility for their own actions. If you complain about someone they have no way of knowing whether you just like to find someone else to blame for your own difficulties.

7. Tell the truth.

But you can be selective with it. Chapter five on *Sample questions and stunning answers* covers this in more detail.

8. Show that you are interested in the job.

The interview is a two-way process. You are here to find out about the job or course and you might not like what you hear. Never mind. Act as if you are really interested. You might change your mind on the train going home, or you may want to apply for another course or job at the same place. If you've behaved as if you're not interested in them, why should they be interested in you next time?

9.   Don't answer a question that you don't understand.

Ask for clarification. Simply say something like, 'Can I check I understand your question?' (then repeat what you understand the question to be). If you haven't a clue what the interviewer was talking about, ask them to rephrase it. If you realise halfway through an answer that you may have misunderstood the question, simply stop and check with the interviewer if this is the case.

10.   Check that you've said enough.

Sometimes there's a long pause after you've spoken. The interviewer may be expecting you to say more. However, only add more if it is relevant to the question.

11.   Let the interviewer know if you have something in common.

If the interviewer happens to mention that they went to the same school as you, you can establish extra rapport by making a simple comment such as 'Was old Mr Jones there then?' Don't overdo it, though.

12.   Don't make comments on sensitive subjects.

Don't mention these subjects unless you have to because of the nature of the course or job you are applying for. These are topics about which people often have strong views. You may well be able to add to the list. Sensitive subjective include race (don't make racist remarks), gender (don't make sexist remarks), politics (theirs may be different), religion (or they may not believe in it) or sexuality.

13.   Speak positively.

Throw positive words into your answers – 'enjoy', 'enthusiastic', etc.

14. Do your homework.

Last – but definitely not least – **prepare thoroughly** by following the guidelines in this book.

> *'We look at everything to do with the student so that we can get a clear overall impression of them as a person. This includes personal things, such as home circumstances.'*

Quote from a college interviewer

Rules for interviewers

This is a heading you didn't expect, but it always helps to understand the other side's viewpoint. Delegates on selection interviewing courses are taught to:

- use open-ended questions. these are questions that are difficult to answer with a simple 'yes' or 'no'
- encourage the candidate to feel at ease
- notice body language
- probe when an answer is unclear or fudged
- use prolonged silence if they think that they're not getting the whole truth – the candidate will almost certainly speak first, and probably tell the interviewer the truth
- be objective
- probe gaps or irregularities in your application form or CV
- look at you as a whole person, not just a total of your skills and qualifications
- do less talking than you – the ratio should be about 20% interviewer speaking, 80% you speaking
- set out the room so that there is no desk between you and them
- have chairs of equal height and quality
- place chairs so that you can see and speak to each other comfortably
- look relaxed, so that you are encouraged to feel the same

Great, except of course that not all interviewers have been on a course and some of them haven't a clue. Which leads us to the worst type of interviewer.

The poor interviewer

Now, if you think you're nervous about being interviewed, spare a thought for the interviewer. Often they're even more frightened than you, especially those people who haven't done much interviewing or who have had no training. This means that they're frightened **and** clueless, which makes it tougher for you. So, what can go wrong and how can you get around it?

Interviewer talks non-stop

This happens surprisingly often. In one way it's a relief – if they're talking, it saves you the bother. The trouble is, you don't get the chance to sell yourself and this type of interviewer is likely to take the last person they interview because they can't remember the others! All this means that you have to make an impression somehow. There are a couple of things you can do.

- Establish rapport with the interviewer by using good non-verbal encouragers, e.g. nodding, saying 'yes, you're right', etc, and getting the odd word in where you can.

- Remember to pick up on any points that you have in common.

Even this sort of interviewer should ask you if you have any questions at the end of the interview. You can use this slot to fill in any information about yourself that you haven't been able to get across before.

The room is poorly laid out

There is little you can do about this, although it is acceptable to move your chair (a little) so that you can see the interviewer(s) more clearly. If you really have to do more than this for some reason, ask permission. Otherwise, you will seem as if you are invading the interviewer's territory.

The interviewer is aggressive

Some, although fortunately not many, interviewers use aggression as a ploy to see how you will cope under pressure. A variation is the 'good cop, bad cop' game, where one interviewer is nice and the other nasty. Keep your cool. Pretend not to notice the aggression. Respond to the questions in an assertive and calm manner.

The interviewer is disorganised

This can include not having prepared for the interview. The interviewer may not have read your application form, CV or record of achievement or Progress File properly or at all. They may not have prepared any questions. They may not know much about the job you are applying for. They may even have lost your papers.

Interviewers sometimes allow interviews to run late. This is very common, especially if you are not the first interviewee of the day. Many interviewers fail to allow sufficient time between interviews and get behind schedule. Some even allow interruptions, which slows down the whole process.

Finally, they may not be making a smooth progression through the interview – darting all over the place with questions.

With all these difficulties, you can make a good impression by keeping calm, being reassuring, looking relaxed (so that the interviewer will 'copy' you), smiling encouragingly.

Andrew's story – the poor interview

'I had an interview at 9am for a job I really wanted. I had a million things to do before I left and it was a great rush, but I made it in time. I was shown into a really grotty waiting room and there I sat for 40 minutes. No one explained what the delay was (although looking back on it, I think they were trying to decide how to run the interview).

Eventually, I was called in and to my horror found it was a group interview – all the candidates doing part of the interview together. No one had warned me about that. I was introduced to all the people who worked in the team. What they didn't tell me was that one of the team members sitting there was applying for the job too. I realised something was odd though, when she kept taking the floor as topics were introduced.

This group interview was followed by an individual interview which was nearly as badly prepared. The questions the interviewer asked were so wide, I didn't know where to start. Fortunately, I had the sense to keep asking questions in return, like "Would you like me to talk about this .... aspect?". The whole thing felt as if they were trying to catch us out: it was pretty unpleasant and I felt really angry. When they phoned to offer me the job I nearly turned it down. One of the first things I did when I started working there was to tell the manager how bad I thought the interview was. To my surprise she agreed, and even apologised.'

The interviewer knows less than you

This can happen if you have a particular area of expertise and are being interviewed by someone who is not directly involved in your type of work, for example, a human resource manager. Likewise, some university or college lecturers interview for subjects other than their own. Never sound condescending if this happens. Remember, the interviewer may not be an expert in your field, but they probably are in their own. You can make the interviewer feel comfortable with their lack of knowledge by simply saying things like 'as you may know ...'.

The interviewer uses words, abbreviations or jargon that you don't understand

Almost every type of work or course has its own abbreviations and jargon and many interviewers will use them unintentionally because they're so used to (what is for them) the short way of saying things. This means that sometimes you won't understand the question that you are being asked. For example, someone applying for a job in a residential home for elderly people might be asked:

'How do you think we should treat EMI clients?'

EMI is short for 'Elderly Mentally Infirm', but not a lot of people know that. (Although perhaps you should have done if you'd done your homework sufficiently.) Don't panic! Simply say:

'That's not an abbreviation I'm familiar with, I'm afraid.'

The interviewer will explain and away you go.

If the interviewer uses a word that you don't understand which is not jargon, see if you can make out the sense from the context – the rest of the sentence. If you're still not sure check it out, make a guess. Rephrase the question and say:

'Can I just be sure I understand the question? Do you mean ...?'

> *'I can't tell you how senior managers don't prepare for the interview. They tell the people about the hours, pay, etc and then dry up. They haven't prepared a single question.'*

> ***Quote from a personnel officer who interviews with senior managers***

First impressions last

As you will see elsewhere in this book, it is suggested that some interviewers make up their minds about a candidate within the first 90 seconds of the interview. Whether or not you are unfortunate enough to come across one of these interviewers, it is vital that your entrance is spot on.

In view of the fact that 90 seconds gives you little time to say much, clearly other factors are at work here. Firstly, there is body language. This is covered in more detail in Chapter 4 *Body language matters*. However, a few pointers on making an entrance with suitable body language are as follows.

- Don't look apologetic – you've been invited to attend the interview and the interviewer(s) really want you there.

- If you're surprised by the layout of the room, try not to show it (some people do!).

- Look at, and smile at, all the people who are present.

- If you shake hands with anyone, shake hands with everyone. Let the interviewer take the initiative here.

- Sit calmly – don't slouch, but don't sit as if there's a poker in your back. It's a good idea to try to sit forward just slightly – it makes you look interested.

- If you have taken anything into the interview room with you (briefcase, etc), put in on the floor beside you, not on your knee

- If you want to take brief notes of any information you will learn, keep a smart notepad and pen ready to hand. Doing this can indeed make you look very professional. If you think the interviewer may feel threatened or uncomfortable about it, simply say, 'Do you mind if I make a few notes about what you're telling me?'.

- Don't put ANYTHING on the interviewer's desk – in animal terms it will be seen as a threat, an invasion of personal space.

- Remember your relaxation techniques, if you need them.

> *'Candidates should always treat everyone in the room equally. On several occasions I have seen candidates assume the women in the room were there to take notes and ignore them. They were actually other managers.'*

Quote from a manager

Secondly, there is dress. This is covered on page 64.

Thirdly, there is that vague thing, rapport. Experienced interviewers know that they have to be careful to avoid the following.

- *The Nimbus effect*' – this is when someone takes a dislike to you because you trigger some negative feeling in them. Almost certainly this will be nothing to do with you, which makes it a bit tough. Perhaps you remind them of their rebellious teenager at home, or your accent takes them back to a bullying school teacher. There's not much you can do in this case. However, you can, lessen the likelihood of it happening by being especially careful about rule no. 12 of the interview game: don't make comments on sensitive subjects. If you make a glib remark about something that the other person holds dear, you're going to have to work awfully hard to overcome their resistance to anything else you say.

(A small extra point: if you've been reading a newspaper on the way to the interview, keep it hidden. If its style or politics aren't the same as the interviewer's, it could trigger the Nimbus effect!)

THE NIMBUS EFFECT

You interact with interviewer

triggers a dubious memory

interviewer notices only bad points

left with poor impression

decreased chances of success

■ *'The Halo effect'* – this is the opposite. In this case the interviewer takes a liking to you because you have something in common or remind them of a person they like. You can tell this sometimes because you get warm feelings coming towards you, and they may make comments about whatever has triggered off their thoughts. You can bask in this goodwill without having to do anything, except – don't blow it!

THE HALO EFFECT

You interact with interviewer

triggers a positive memory

interviewer notices only good points

has favourable impressions

increased chance of success

Lastly, there is your voice. Even in 90 seconds, you'll have time to say a few words. Use those 'settling in' questions to test your voice in the room. A big room usually requires more projection of your voice (but not shouting). However, there is no 'hard and fast' rule, except to try your voice in the room and be aware of the need to pitch it correctly. If you are not sure of this, or if people have told you in the past that you have a quiet or loud voice, it would be a good idea to practise (with the help of a friend to listen) in rooms of different sizes.

If you are applying for a job, university or college place in another part of the country to your own, don't worry about accent (unless it's so thick that others can't understand you). However, do try not to use 'dialect words' if possible, because the interviewer may not know what you're talking about. (Dialect words are those which have a meaning or a different meaning in a particular area. For example: children living in the south of England have 'pocket money'; children in the north of England have 'spends'.)

> '*The interviewer showed me to my chair, sat opposite me and then said, 'Will you take the pens out of your top pocket please. I've got a thing about pens in top pockets.' Phew! I didn't quite know how to react, whether it was a joke or not. It wasn't.'*

Quote from a man applying for a sales job

Making an exit

So, you've done a great job throughout the interview. Let's see how you can crown that achievement. Here are a few tips:

- smile at all the interviewers

- thank them for seeing you

- have a great parting line prepared such as:

'Thank you for the interview, I'm sure if you give me this job, you will be very satisfied with my work.'

'Thank you for the interview, I'm sure that if you give me a place on the course, you won't be disappointed by my performance.'

- taking the lead from the interviewer, shake hands if appropriate

- gather your bits and pieces tidily

- smile again, and leave the room, closing the door gently but firmly behind you

- let out a sigh of relief and pat yourself on the back.

There, that was okay, wasn't it? If you think the parting line is a bit over the top, think again. Say it honestly and sincerely – they'll love it!

Chapter checklist

Do you:

- know what to expect when you walk into the interview room?

- feel familiar with a typical interview structure?

- understand the unwritten rules of the interview for yourself and the interviewer(s)?

- feel ready for the unprepared or poor interviewer?

- feel confident that you can handle jargon, abbreviations, etc?

- feel able to ask if you don't understand a question properly?

- know the first impression you make on people?

- feel comfortable with sitting down, placing your briefcase, etc tidily?

- feel able to manage silence effectively?

- know how to get in those good points about yourself which may not have arisen during questioning?

- know a great final line as you finish your interview?

Chapter three
Preparation, preparation, preparation

You should read this chapter:

- as soon as you begin thinking about applying for a job or university/college place. It will be of help also when you are completing an application form or your CV

- if you are preparing for a specific interview.

By the end of this chapter you should know:

- what interviewers are looking for in candidates

- how to evaluate your skills

- how to use background material to help you prepare for the interview

- how interviewers 'score' candidates

- how to keep calm during the interview

- how to have a mock interview.

To fail to prepare is to prepare to fail

Interviewers say that less than a quarter of people that they interview have prepared properly for it. This means that if you do the right preparation you will be streets ahead of the competition.

'I just interviewed 16 people, not one of them had bothered to really understand what our organisation does before they came. Hopeless!'

Quote from a human resources manager

Job, university or college interviews

There are a few basic differences between university/college and job interviews. Universities and colleges interview many people because they have several places on offer and have to allow for students decisions to accept a place elsewhere. This is not true of job interviews. Usually, employers are filling only one vacancy and it is rare that they will interview more than about eight people. In times of high unemployment they may select the eight from the many application forms they have received. In times of full employment they may be scratching around to find a decent number of people to interview.

Either way, once you have been offered a job interview, the odds in your favour have already narrowed impressively. If you are invited for interview, you must have convinced the organisation that you are a good potential candidate. Interviewers do not waste their time interviewing people who have no chance of success.

What the interviewer wants

In a nutshell, the interviewer wants you to say enough about yourself for him or her (or them) to decide whether you are suitable for the job or university/college place. This sounds obvious, but in fact there is some research that shows that interviews are not at all reliable in predicting people's ability to do a job, or their success on a course. Nevertheless, there are very few organisations willing to take the chance of going ahead without one.

University and college interviewers are looking for people with the right qualifications who can convince them that they'll turn up to at least a few lectures they'll complete the course (drop-out rates don't look good to prospective students); they'll pass (high failure rates don't reflect well on the lecturers or the institution); they really know the course details (so don't get them mixed up with a course at another college).

However, people interviewing for jobs are also looking for the necessary skills, knowledge and personality to do the job effectively.

All of this means that you need to know what is expected of you in these areas and that means preparation.

So, how do you get started? Well, the preparation you need for your application form will be a great place to begin because you will have done some of the ground work already. If you want to read more about this, *CVs and Applications* by Patricia McBride (Lifetime Careers Publishing, 2004) is just what you need.

Research the organisation, university or college

Firstly, research the organisation, university or college. You can do this by:

- reading any material that is sent to you

- looking at the organisation's website and reading it thoroughly, making notes on any relevant areas

- asking people who may have knowledge of the organisation, college or university

- looking in local or national newspapers for current issues regarding the organisation or course you want to study.

Secondly, research the job or course. Read carefully any material that you are sent. If invited to do so, telephone the contact person to ask any questions that you may have. Try to talk to people who have done similar jobs or taken similar courses. This will help you to ask intelligent questions and give informed answers at interview.

'I like to see candidates who have worked as hard at preparing for the interview as I have.'

Quote from a human resources manager

Industry/organisation knowledge for jobs

As preparation for your interview, find out as much as you can about the challenges faced by the industry or organisation and the company's financial state (look at their company accounts on the internet, ask in your reference library and keep an eye on the press). Also, find out what's new in the industry or organisation and anything else about the company that you should know (such as mergers, takeovers, new ranges, etc. Again, keep an eye on the press and professional journals, if appropriate).

You may be asked questions about these topics at interview. In addition to the information sources above, once you are invited to interview you could telephone and ask for company newsletters, and annual accounts if it is a limited company.

Your skills evaluation

Many people are unsure how to go about evaluating their skills, but it is quite simple once you know how. Skills fall into categories – you will need to consider each category and measure your abilities:

Cognitive skills – this is traditional intelligence, the ability to think things through in your mind and work out logical answers and solutions.

Practical skills – the ability to perform tasks with your hands.

Communication skills – the ability to communicate clearly with others.

Emotional intelligence (EI) skills – this is an area of increasing importance to companies. Emotional intelligence is about being aware of your emotions and being able to use and control them enough to get along with other people and on with your job. Employers realise that people with low EI are often difficult employees, because while it is relatively easy to teach practical skills, it is more difficult to teach EI skills.

Activity

Imagine that you have been out of work since leaving school six months ago. You haven't been idle though. You've done all the housework, shopping and cooking for the family and minded your little sister after school. What skills have you used? You can find suggestions below.

You can do the same sort of activity for anything you have been doing. For example:

- any kind of work you have done in the past

- voluntary work (including informal work)

- studying

- club or team membership or leadership.

Activity answers

You have been doing the shopping, housework and cooking for your family as well as looking after your little sister after school. Assuming that you've been making a good job of it, here are some of the skills that you may have used:

- Budgeting – for the shopping

- Reliability – collecting your sister from school, having meals ready

- Observation – noticing the dirt and dealing with it

- Patience – dealing with the sister

- Organisation – to get everything done

- Prioritising – deciding what to do and when

- Time management – fitting everything into the time allowed, and still getting to the school gates

- Motivation – getting yourself going

- Message-taking – when people knock on the door or the telephone rings

- Honesty – not stealing the milk money!

I'm sure you can think of others, but this will give you some ideas.

Continue analysing your skills in this way until you are confident that you have listed them all. Now you are ready to prepare yourself for your own big chance to convince the interviewer that you are the best thing since sliced bread…

Skills, qualifications and knowledge are important but they are not the complete answer. Interviewers are looking for other things too.

Activity

What the interviewer wants

Put yourself in the interviewer's position. Imagine that you are about to interview someone for a job or college place. You will be spending perhaps a whole day interviewing up to eight people. You've done a good job at the preparation stage. You have carefully considered all the application forms and are sure that those people invited for interview have the necessary skills and qualifications. What, then, are you looking for?

Keeping in mind the interview that you are preparing for, write a list of ten things that you think the interviewer may be seeking. These should be general points and not skills or qualification-specific. Keep your answers in your interview file. Look at them before each interview to refresh your memory. Remember, the list may need changing for each interview.

Activity answers

Here are some suggestions. You may have thought of other things:

- someone who will fit in with the existing work or student group

- someone who is clean and reasonably tidy

- someone who is likeable

- someone who is not overqualified (or they may get bored and leave quickly)

- someone who is clear about what they want from the job and the organisation or college/course

- someone who is clear about what they can offer the organisation or college/course

- someone who speaks well and gets points across clearly

- someone who has thought about how they can use their existing skills and knowledge, even if they are not exactly the same as those required in the job or course on offer.

- someone who knows what they want in the future

- someone who is flexible.

In his book *Great Answers to Tough Interview Questions* (Kogan Page 1998), Martin John Yate takes this further. He lists (see below) a number of personal and professional qualities that employers seek. The good news is that you can have all these qualities without having had a single job.

Personal qualities

- drive – knowing where you're going, having the energy to get there

- motivation – getting on without supervision, being willing to find out how to do things

- communication skills – this can include both the written and spoken word

- chemistry – the ability to get on with people

- energy – having plenty of 'get-up-and-go'

- determination – someone with stamina, who sees a job through to the end

- confidence – assertiveness, not looking down on anyone or being intimidated by people in authority.

Professional qualities

- reliability - being dependable

- honesty and integrity – essential; no one likes to be around people that they can't trust. People will appreciate knowing where they are with you; it doesn't mean you have to be blunt, but you have to be assertive and honest in your dealings with others

- pride – taking pride in yourself and your work

- dedication – putting that bit of extra effort into your work

- analytical skills – an ability to step back and look at a problem from various angles

- listening skills – really hearing what people are saying. Taking account of the difference between what is said and what is meant.

Personal competence – emotional intelligence and how we manage ourselves

- having emotional awareness – recognising your emotions and the effects that they have on you

- having accurate self-assessment – knowing your strengths and weaknesses

- having strategies for continuous self-improvement

- being self-confident – having a sense of your own worth and abilities.

Self-regulation

- having self-control – being in control of unhelpful emotions and impulses

- being trustworthy – having honesty and integrity

- being conscientious – taking responsibility for yourself and your performance

- being adaptable – being flexible in handling the ups and downs of life

- being innovative – thinking creatively, accepting new ideas

- being in control of your moods.

Motivation

- to do with being able to reach goals

- striving for achievement – a drive to reach excellence

- being committed – working towards a goal and within the framework required by the college or organisation

- having initiative – a willingness to use opportunities as they arise

- being optimistic – not feeling overcome when things don't go to plan.

Empathy

- being aware of the feelings and needs of others

- understanding other people – sensing their feelings and taking interest in them

- developing other people – encouraging others to reach their potential

- being customer-focused – anticipating and meeting customer needs

- accepting diversity – gaining through the differences between people

- political awareness – understanding how the organisation works.

Social skills

- communicating effectively with others

- influencing others – using effective skills to persuade others
- communicating effectively – listening clearly and communicating clearly
- managing conflict – negotiating and resolving disagreements
- leadership – inspiring individuals and groups
- managing change – or initiating it
- having good relationships – building relationships that benefit everyone
- working cooperatively – rather than competitively
- working in a team – working towards collective goals.

A reminder – these are highly prized qualities, so do think if you can offer examples of them.

Remember, interviewers want everyone who walks through the door to be able to do the job or to succeed on the course. They want to have a hard time making a choice. This means that they are on your side. They are not out to trip you up, make you feel silly or show you how inadequate you are. They want you to be good.

Activity

Look through Yate's list (pages 43-46) and think about how you could show an interviewer that you had each quality. It's not enough to just say that you have this quality, you need to think of an example to back up what you are saying. What examples could you give?

The truth, the whole truth and nothing but the truth?

During an interview you should always tell the truth. If you lie and are found out you could lose the job or place offer. However, there are ways and ways of telling the truth. This is one of the well-recognised rules of the interview game.

For example, supposing you have three main hobbies – reading, seeing friends and music. The job you are going for requires you to be very sociable, but you actually spend quite a bit of your time alone reading or playing music. You don't emphasise that. You talk about your other, quite genuine hobby – seeing friends.

So, tell the truth, but use it to highlight those strengths you possess that will help you to succeed at the interview.

Preparing for questions

The actual question and answer session is usually the part of the interview that people feel least confident about handling well. Luckily, with preparation you can anticipate almost every question that you're likely to be asked. Chapter six *Awkward questions, brilliant answers*, gives you sample questions and answers, so this chapter gives you general points in order to help you anticipate what questions you might be asked.

The type of questions asked will depend on a number of things, such as the course content or requirements of the job. Also relevant will be the style and experience of the interviewer and whether the organisation has an equal opportunities policy. It is almost certain that you will be asked about what you said in your application form.

'Basically, we ask everyone the same questions, but add one or two extras depending on what's in their application form.'

Quote from a college lecturer

Using your background material

You can work out pretty much all of the questions that you are likely to be asked beforehand by doing a bit of research. Your research areas are going to be:

- yourself
- the organisation or college
- the job or course
- topical issues around the job or course topic.

Researching yourself

Earlier in this chapter we looked at ways to analyse your strengths, weaknesses and abilities. You should do this specifically keeping in mind the job or course in which you are interested. Other material that will help you includes:

- your record of achievement, Progress File or General National Vocational Qualification (GNVQ) portfolio

- your CV or application form

- the job description and person specification (or competencies) for a job

- the course and college or university details.

Information about organisations, universities and colleges can be found by:

- asking around, especially if the organisation is local

- reading local or national newspapers

- asking your personal/careers adviser

- asking your library what information they have – companies have to keep financial records and these and other information may well be available at your library. There is a list of suitable sources of information at the back of this book

- surfing the internet – many companies and colleges have their own web pages

- knowing about current issues in the area of your choice (e.g. if you are applying to medical school, consider the changes in the NHS – the interviewer will expect you to have at least some knowledge of them)

- reading trade/professional magazines or journals.

If you are applying for a university or college place you should have a good idea about the course for which you have applied. Also, you should have (or have found out) some information about the locality.

If you are applying for a job, you should have received from the organisation a job description, a person specification and information about the organisation. They may also send you information about the organisation. Some job descriptions and/or person specifications state whether each item is an essential or desirable quality that they want the candidate to have.

To make the most effective use of all these documents, you should go through them and underline those words which appear to be most important. Once you have done this, it is not difficult to work out the sort of questions that you might be asked.

Here is a sample job description and person specification for a sales assistant position in a fashion shop. Significant words have been underlined.

Job description

Job title: Sales Assistant

Responsible to: Stores Manager

Duties

1. To ensure that the shop is tidy before opening time each morning.

2. To assist customers with requests about merchandise.

3. To staff the tills as necessary.

4. To staff the changing rooms as necessary.

5. To keep the shop and merchandise tidy at all times.

6. To answer the telephone.

Person specification

This person specification lists the criteria necessary for the person we seek to appoint.

a. Fashionably dressed in a way that's appropriate to the nature of the store.

b. Clean and tidy.

c. Able to work unsupervised.

d. Able to think ahead and make decisions.

e. Experience at staffing tills.

f. Experience at answering the telephone.

g. Willingness to work as part of a team.

h. Non-smoker or willing not to smoke during working hours.

i. Experience at selling.

j. Customer service experience.

Items (a), (b), (g) and (h) are essential. Other items are desirable.

Activity

Below are a job description and person specification for a clerk/ typist vacancy with a company that provides training courses. Look at these documents and highlight or underline those words which you consider to be important clues to what you will be expected to be able to do, or qualities the interviewer will be looking for.

Job description

Job title: Clerk/Typist

Post no: 234

Scale: A/B

Responsible to: Office manager

Main purpose of job

To support the office manager and her secretary in the day-to-day running of the training section.

Specific duties

1. To undertake typing for the office manager as instructed by the senior secretary.

2. To keep the office filing up-to-date.

3. To act as relief receptionist during holiday periods.

4. To keep the training library tidy and ensure that all resource material is checked out and returned on time.

5. To proofread newly-developed course material.

6. To book venues and catering for courses.

Person specification

Job title: Clerk/Typist

The following person specification lists the criteria applicable to the person we seek to recruit for the above post.

a.	Ability to type at least 35wpm	E
b.	Good attention to detail	E
c.	Telephone answering skills	D
d.	Good organisational skills	E
e.	Ability to work unsupervised	D
f.	Knowledge of training business	D
g.	Knowledge of wordprocessing	E
h.	Knowledge of desktop publishing	D
i.	Good level of English	E
j.	Non-smoker	E

D = Desirable criteria   E = Essential criteria

Activity answers

You should have underlined the following words in the job description and person specification.

Job description

Job Title: Clerk/Typist

Post No: 234

Scale: A/B

Responsible to: Office manager

Main purpose of job

To support the office manager and her secretary in the day-to-day running of the training section.

Specific duties

1. To undertake typing for the office manager as instructed by the senior secretary.

2. To keep the office filing up-to-date.

3. To act as relief receptionist during holiday periods.

4. To keep the training library tidy and ensure that all resource material is checked out and returned on time.

5. To proofread newly developed course material.

6. To book venues and catering for courses.

Person specification

Job title: Clerk/Typist

The following person specification lists the criteria applicable to the person we seek to recruit for the above post.

a. <u>Ability to type at least 35wpm</u>   E

b. Good <u>attention to detail</u>   E

c. <u>Telephone answering</u> skills   D

d. Good <u>organisational skills</u>   E

e. Ability to <u>work unsupervised</u>   D

f. <u>Knowledge of training business</u>   D

g. Knowledge of <u>wordprocessing</u>   E

h. Knowledge of <u>desktop publishing</u>   D

i. Good level of <u>English</u>   E

j. <u>Non-smoker</u>   E

D = Desirable criteria   E = Essential criteria

With this person specification you may well have underlined everything, as they are all important.

Taking the items one at a time, it is clear that the interviewer will ask questions about:

Skills – typing, filing, telephone, organisation, general office skills

Education – to ensure that you have a reasonable standard of English

Knowledge – of the training business (you should have looked this up if you didn't know about this beforehand)

Attitude – ability to work unsupervised, to be polite to customers, willingness to learn, etc.

In fact, this is the type of activity that you should have undertaken before you completed the application form or amended your CV when applying for the job.

By doing this you will see where your own skills, qualifications and experience match with the information provided. Don't worry if there is not an exact match. Early in your career, it is unlikely that you will have had an opportunity to gain a wide range of experience. Employers will be looking to see whether you have any transferable skills or experience. That is, experience in similar areas which suggest an appropriate aptitude. Also, you will need to consider transferable skills and knowledge if you are applying for a university or college place that is not directly linked to your qualifications. Armed with all this information, you can begin to work out the questions that you are likely to be asked and how you might answer them. This is covered in much more detail in chapters five and six, but the following activity will give you a head start.

Activity

Imagine that you are going to interview someone for the clerk/typist job we've just looked at. Using the job description and person specification provided, write down as many interview questions as you can think of.

Activity answers

Some questions which might be asked at this interview for a clerk/typist are as follows.

1. What experience do you have that is relevant to this post?

2. How fast can you type?

3. What wordprocessing packages are you familiar with?

4. Give me an example of your organisational skills.

5. How do you manage your time?

6. What qualities do you think are important in a receptionist?

7. How would you organise booking venues for courses?

8. What do you know about business training?

9. What experience do you have of desktop publishing?

10. Give me an example of your attention to fine detail.

11. How do you think you will manage if you have to work unsupervised?

12. How do you make decisions?

When you are applying for any college place or job, this is the process you should go through. The time you spend will be well rewarded with your increased confidence and ability at interview.

> *'I reckon less than 25% of 16-year-olds I see prepare for the interview. Sometimes when I ask them why they want to do this (continuous assessment) course they say, "because I don't cope well with the pressure of exams." Unbelievable!'*

> **Quote from a BTEC lecturer**

Preparing to keep your cool

Nerves can help you during an interview – a bit of extra adrenalin is just what you need to keep you sharp. But too much fear (and too much adrenalin) has the opposite effect. So you need to work on eliminating (or at least lessening) those unwanted feelings. Luckily, just as you can prepare for any other aspect of an interview, you can prepare yourself to keep calm.

Visualisation techniques

Amazingly, by changing the pictures in your mind, you can change how you feel and behave – sports people have known this for years. Here are a few techniques. They all have three things in common. First, they distract you momentarily from stressful feelings. Secondly, they allow you to slow down your breathing (most people breath more shallowly and faster when they are nervous). Finally, they give you back a feeling of control.

Select the one which you think might work best for you and practise until the calming reaction becomes automatic. Practice is the key. It is no good leaving it until the interview itself to use one of these techniques. Although it may well help, if you rehearse the method thoroughly in advance it will have a far greater impact.

To do this practice, select a safe place and time and begin to think about a stressful situation (the interview?), watch a horror film, or seek out a spider or whatever turns you off. Then use one of the techniques to calm yourself. Really try to capture the feeling of being in control of yourself and the situation. Slow your breathing, sit in a more upright way, feel strong, feel personally powerful. Feel good about yourself. If you do this enough times, the calming reaction becomes automatic and you can 'switch into' calm mode whenever necessary.

If you're a bit sceptical about this, remember that you weren't born being nervous of interviews. You learned to react in a certain way because of circumstances combined with your personality. In the same way, you can unlearn these nuisance feelings, leaving you feeling in control. It works, try it!

'Often people are so nervous that they don't hear my questions properly. This means that they waffle on, missing the point entirely.'

Quote from a manager with extensive interviewing experience

Calming technique 1 – produce your own show

When we dread something, there can be a tendency to mentally rehearse it going wrong. We picture all the ghastly things than can happen and imagine them in vivid detail. This is bad news. So let's change all that.

When we do something, it causes a chain of chemical reactions in the brain. The more we do it, the thicker the chain gets until we automatically have the same response to the same situation. This means we lose flexibility and ability to choose from a range of possible options for behaviour.

Interestingly, when we imagine something, we also set a chain of chemical reactions going in the brain. And the more we imagine that same thing, the thicker the chain gets. So, if you replace a negative image with a positive image and imagine it often enough, your brain will take you automatically along the positive path.

Obviously, you will want wonderful positive images of yourself at interview. So sit quietly and imagine a television screen. Now, imagine a production of your interview, and as you do so remember that you are the producer. You can edit the picture as often as you like until you are happy with the finished result.

When you're happy with the picture, make it bigger and brighter and then, if you can, 'step into' the picture and imagine yourself really there. Get into that positive feeling of being so confident and in control of yourself during the interview.

Practise this picture over and over again until you realise that your feelings about the interview are really positive. Each rehearsal will only take a few minutes, and think of all you have to gain. It works...

Relaxation technique 2 – anchoring

This is a great technique, very simple and effective. With one hand, hold your other wrist, and as you do so insert gentle pressure with one finger or your thumb. As you do so, say slowly to yourself 'calm, calm', and become aware of your breathing. Slow your breathing down. Feel in control. Practise this in a quiet time – always using pressure from the same finger or thumb – and do it often enough so that the link is made naturally between touching your wrist and calming down. During the interview, if you realise you are feeling a bit nervous you can simply repeat this process and you will feel much calmer.

Do try this one, it has several advantages. Barring amputation, you will always have your wrist with you and the action is very unobtrusive. Also, you can hold your wrist comfortably whether sitting down, standing up or holding documents.

Be careful, of course, that you don't grip your wrist too tightly. As with the other examples here, you can learn to associate this technique with feeling calm by using the method described above.

By the way, you don't have to say 'calm' – it can be anything that works for you. Some of the suggestions in the section below might be effective for you.

Relaxation technique 3 – positive self-talk

If you are feeling panicky, it's likely that all sorts of negative feelings and thoughts are going through your mind:

- 'Help, I'm going to be sick!'

- 'I'll make a right mess of this.'

- 'What if I can't answer the questions?'

- 'Why did this big zit have to come up today of all days?'

- 'Why am I here?'

These are all perfectly natural. The thing to remember is that you can take control of these feelings. After all, if you're not in control of your mind, who is?

So, start adjusting your self-talk. Stop the negative thoughts and replace them with positive ones instead:

- 'I can handle this.'

- 'Interviews are a good opportunity for me to find out about the college (job).'

- 'They don't want me to fail, and I won't.'

- 'I feel good today. I'm in control.'

- 'I'm an okay person.'

As you think these positive thoughts, adjust your body language. Negative thoughts tend to mean that we slump. Lift your head, square your shoulders and take a few deep breaths. You'll be surprised at how changing your body language changes your mood. It's okay – it'll be all right, you can do it.

In fact, you could get the interviewer on your side by owning up to your nervousness, so long as you don't dwell on it. If you feel really nervous and think that you look like a quivering wreck, own up. Simply say, briefly, 'I always feel nervous during interviews' and then carry on with what you were saying.

INNER SELF-TALK

Negative self-talk

poor self-image

'loser' body language and lack of confidence in interview

weak performance at interview

Positive self-talk

strong self-image

'winner' body language, and confidence in interview

good performance at interview

Relaxation technique 4 – grounding

Grounding is a bit like anchoring. The idea is to distract your thoughts away from the stressful situation towards a calm feeling. With this technique, you deliberately become conscious of your body weight through the seat of the chair or through your feet. Try it now as you read this page. You don't usually think about it, but it's easy once you focus your attention.

Once you've become conscious of your body weight (not how fat you are!), think to yourself 'calm, calm', slow down your breathing and take control again.

Relaxation technique 5 – visualising

This is a great one if you're good at fantasies. In your minds' eye, conjure up a soothing picture. It might be a lovely scene from a holiday, a flower, a waterfall, whatever. It's a good idea to choose a picture that includes some gently rippling water – very soothing. With this image firmly in your mind, if only for a split second, slow down your breathing and think to yourself 'calm, calm', or hear the beautiful sounds that go with the picture. Take control, breath more slowly, allow the tension to go, and you'll feel on top of the situation.

When you practise using this technique, concentrate on the soothing quality of your chosen image to help you feel calm.

At the interview, if you realise that you are feeling nervous, simply imagine your calming picture and you will feel more in control.

Visualisation technique 6 – imagining

This is one that you've probably learned from your granny:
Imagine the interviewer in his or her underwear.
It's a wonderful leveller, and they won't seem nearly so imposing without the posh business suit.

My granny used to remind me as well, 'Just remember, they all go to the toilet the same as us' – another great leveller.

Try it now! What you have got to lose but your fear? You'll feel a little foolish the first few times, but if you practise when you're alone, no one will know.

Practical matters

So far we've looked at mental and emotional preparation for the interview. Let's look now at more practical matters. You have been invited to attend an interview. What do you need to consider?

The place

- Do you know where the university, college or organisation is?

- How will you get there?

- If you need to use public transport, what bus or train do you have to catch?

- What is the timetable?

- How long will it take to get there?

- If you are driving, can you use their car park? (phone first if you're not sure).

Remember to allow yourself plenty of travel time. The last thing you want is to spend the journey anxiously looking at your watch and feeling panicky. And a definite minus point in most interviewers' books is to arrive late. After all, if you do that at an interview what would you be like once you got the job or a place on that course?

What to take

You may have been asked to take some things with you, for example, proof of qualifications, references or proof that you can work in this country.

There may be some other things that you would like to take. For job interviews, these might include:

- your application form, CV, record of achievement, Progress File, certificates

- your list of questions to ask at the end of the interview

- details about the organisation – so that you can re-read them if you're kept waiting or on the journey.

For a university or college interview, you should definitely take:

- your record of achievement, Progress File, certificates

- samples of any appropriate work

- details of the course and university or college.

Also, for either type of interview you should prepare everyday things:

Checklist
Item

Handkerchief or clean tissues

Specs (if you need them)

Money

Mobile phone – with enough credit for emergencies

Timetable or parking instructions

Umbrella (if there's the least chance of rain)

A comb

The name and telephone number of the interviewer, in case of delays.

And for women:

Spare tights/stockings

Sanitary protection.

Overnight stays

Many interviews, especially for college places, will involve travelling to another part of the country. What does this involve? Well, imagine yourself in a strange town, one hour before the interview, discovering that the only shoes you've got to wear with your smart outfit are your trainers. Doesn't bear thinking about, does it?

So planning is key. Make a list of **everything** that you're likely to need a couple of days before you set out (this gives you time to buy or borrow any missing items).

First impressions last

So here you are, well organised. You know where you're going, how to get there and what you need to take. Now you have to decide what to wear.

Many experts on interviewer training say that the interviewer unconsciously decides within the first 90 seconds whether or not they like a candidate. Then they spend the rest of the interview justifying their decision. As one college lecturer said: 'We're looking at the whole person and dress presents part of the overall pattern. If they dress untidily, it may mean they think untidily.'

'I interviewed one woman who turned up in a pink fluffy trouser suit. She'd have only needed ears to look like a toy bunny!'

Quote from a manager

Also, keep in mind that many interviewers are not trained, and that many of them are walking bags of prejudices. Unfortunately, there is nothing you can do about this from outside the organisation, but once you've a place on the course or the job that you want, you can work to change things from the inside.

'But,' you may be thinking, 'I don't have many clothes and no money to buy more.' Do the best you can with what you have. Look through your possible outfits, keeping in mind, 'What does the sort of person who already does the job or attend the course I'm looking for choose to wear?' This doesn't matter quite so much for students, although you should still make sure you look clean and tidy!

Looking right is very important. The comments below relate more to job interviews. For example, if you're going for a job as a garage mechanic and you're lucky enough to have a £500 suit complete with silk tie and mobile phone, you might look a bit over the top. No interviewer wants to feel inferior beside the candidate!

So, dress smartly and neatly. This is no time for extremes of fashion (unless you're going for a job where it's appropriate, such as in a trendy fashion shop). You need to look sensible, reliable and, above all, employable.

Appearance matters

Now you've looked at your wardrobe and selected the best that you can. Whatever you choose, inspect it carefully. Are any repairs needed? Is it clean? It's no good noticing as you dress for the big occasion that it has a gravy stain down the front. Get the outfit ready well in advance, and remember:

- look clean and tidy

- have your shoes polished and repaired, even if they're old

- have clean hair

- smell okay – no body odour or bad breath

- don't overdo the perfume or aftershave

- look appropriate for the season – I once interviewed someone who was wearing a very thick tartan suit on a very hot summer day – for this and other reasons she didn't get the job.

Mum's the word – or is she?

While it's rare for young people to take their parents along to a job interview, sometimes they do take them to a college interview, especially at higher education colleges, and also to work-based learning interviews. There's nothing right or wrong about this, but you may want to give it some thought.

'About 50% of them bring their parents along to the interview. I've forgotten who's applying for the course and interviewed parents instead.'

Quote from a college lecturer

Yes, it's sad but true that interviewers are human and get it wrong occasionally, like forgetting to speak to you when a parent is there. So when considering whether to take along a parent keep in mind the following.

- Will you cringe when your friends see their old-fashioned clothes?

- Are they domineering types who won't let you get a word in edgeways?

- Do they think they know more than the lecturer about the subject?

On a more serious note, if you do take a parent along, discuss with them beforehand what their role is to be and remember to introduce them to your interviewer. It is awkward for interviewers who are faced with you plus parent(s) to have to ask or guess who is actually going into the interview room. Furthermore, if a parent is going into the interview room with you, decide whether they are going to sit silently unless they are asked to comment, or whether they can feel free to join in.

The mock interview

If you feel unsure about interviews, then you need to rehearse. It's just a skill like any other – and skills need practice. So, do a mock interview. Here are the steps to take:

- Find someone who has some experience of being an interviewer and who will be able to give you some honest feedback. In advance, give them the information about the job or college that you have received from the organisation and the list of questions that you don't want to be asked.

- Ask them to work out a list of questions that they think you might be asked. If they don't know enough about your particular specialism, tell them what questions you expect.

- Try to get the use of a video camera. Set it up on a tripod or table, so that you can just leave it there, turn it on, and forget about it. Remember to have it focused on you, not the interviewer.

- Wear your interview outfit so that you begin to feel comfortable in it and can see what it looks like to others.

- Start the mock interview outside the door. Knock and let the 'interviewer' let you in. Remember the 'Halo' and 'Nimbus' effects. You need to see what effect you have in the first vital moments. Continue through the interview. Don't worry if you fluff a question – that's why you're here, it's just practice. Stop the tape. Think about how you can answer the question, start the tape and continue.

- Do all the sections of the interview, including asking your questions at the end, and leaving the room after your final brilliant line.

- Have a cup of tea.

- Review the interview and tape with your 'interviewer'.

To help you give some structure to looking at the tape, or discussing your interview if you haven't been able to record it, there are checklists on the next few pages. If you can, get this photocopied and enlarged and have two copies done, one for each of you.

Before you start discussing the interview, both of you should make notes on how you think it went. This can be particularly helpful because we often have the wrong impression of our performance and you can literally compare notes.

Ask your interviewer to be specific. If he or she has said, 'Didn't look confident', ask for detailed information. What made you seem unconfident? Your tone of voice? Hesitant answers? Body language? (if so what body language?) You need answers that you can use, so vague comments won't do.

Be persistent: Keep asking, 'If that was good, what made it good so that I can do it again?' or, 'If that wasn't right, what should I do differently to make it better?' Pin them down until you feel absolutely confident that you now know what behaviour to change to improve your performance.

If you really think that the other person is wrong about some aspect of how you handled the interview, ask another to look at the tape, or practise the interview again with someone else. See if you get the same feedback.

Interviewing skills checklist

On the scale 1-10, please circle the number which you feel reflects how well the inteviewee performed and then state what they did well or could do differently.

How appropriately was the interviewee dressed?
1   2   3   4   5   6   7   8   9   10
What was good/could be changed?

How good was the interviewee's entrance?
1   2   3   4   5   6   7   8   9   10
What was good/could be changed?

How well did the interviewee settle in the chair, remembering to put belongings aside/keep notebook to hand?
1   2   3   4   5   6   7   8   9   10
What was good/could be changed?

Did the interviewee smile when settling down?
1   2   3   4   5   6   7   8   9   10
What was good/could be changed?

Did the interviewee establish rapport quickly?
1   2   3   4   5   6   7   8   9   10
What was good/could be changed?

Did the interviewee sell him/herself well, but without sounding boastful?
1   2   3   4   5   6   7   8   9   10
What was good/could be changed?

Did the interviewee answer question 1 convincingly?
1   2   3   4   5   6   7   8   9   10
What was good/could be changed?

Did the interviewee answer question 2 convincingly?
1   2   3   4   5   6   7   8   9   10
What was good/could be changed?

Did the interviewee manage the right degree of friendliness?
1   2   3   4   5   6   7   8   9   10
What was good/could be changed?

Was the interviewee's attitude positive?

1   2   3   4   5   6   7   8   9   10

What was good/could be changed?

Did the interviewee maintain appropriate eye contact?

1   2   3   4   5   6   7   8   9   10

What was good/could be changed?

Did the interviewee use appropriate body language?

1   2   3   4   5   6   7   8   9   10

What was good/could be changed?

Did the interviewee display any distracting mannerisms?

1   2   3   4   5   6   7   8   9   10

What was good/could be changed?

Did the interviewee display knowledge of the organisation/college and current issues?

1   2   3   4   5   6   7   8   9   10

What was good/could be changed?

How well did the interviewee show enthusiasm?

1   2   3   4   5   6   7   8   9   10

What was good/could be changed?

Did the interviewee have a great final line?

1   2   3   4   5   6   7   8   9   10

What was good/could be changed?

Did the interviewee make a good exit?

1   2   3   4   5   6   7   8   9   10

What was good/could be changed?

Did the interviewee ask appropriate questions at the end of the interview?

1   2   3   4   5   6   7   8   9   10

What was good/could be changed?

General comments on interviewee's performance

Remember, you can ask the interviewer to use an interview score sheet similar to the one on page 24.

Chapter checklist

Have you:

- researched the university, college or organisation?

- researched the job or course?

- studied yourself and how you fit the job description or course requirements?

- understood how interviewers will score you?

- practised some calming methods?

- considered practical issues, such as travel arrangements?

- conducted a mock interview?

Chapter four
Body language matters

You should read this chapter:

■ two or three days prior to the interview.

By the end of this chapter you should know:

■ the importance of being consistent with your verbal and non-verbal communication

■ typical body language signals

■ how to look calm and composed

■ how to 'read' the interviewer

■ which signals tell the interviewer that you have something to hide.

It ain't what you say, it's the way that you say it...

You may think that the words you use are the most important aspect of communication, but you'd be wrong. Imagine the scene: you sit in the interview looking at the floor and wringing your hands nervously. 'Yes', you say, 'I'm a very confident person and I can easily deal with difficult situations at work.' I don't think so.

In fact, the communication we have with others is to do with much more than words alone. Look at this pie chart:

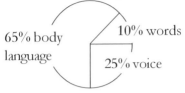

Broken down, the message that others receive from us (and that we receive from them) is transmitted mostly by body language – a staggering 65%. Of the message 25% is to do with your voice (tone, pitch, etc) and only 10% includes the words themselves. So, here you are, with your questions and answers wonderfully prepared and you can still blow it.

> *'One man came in and sat on his hands throughout the whole interview. Literally. At one stage when he became enthusiastic, he actually bounced up and down on his hands. I was working so hard at not laughing I had trouble concentrating on what he was saying.'*

Quote from an experienced interviewer

The good news is that most people display body language which is no problem at all, and you're probably one of those people. Nevertheless, trained interviewers will be on the lookout for what your non-verbal signals are saying, so you need to know what they are looking for.

One important point to keep in mind is that no one piece of body language should be taken in isolation, you need to see a cluster of gestures to assess what's really going on in someone's mind. For this reason, experienced interviewers will not interview with a desk between you and them – they'll want to be able to see the whole of you, right down to your toes! Why? Read on and all will be revealed.

Ethnic differences

The information in this chapter is based on mainstream British body language. One of the difficulties about the whole subject is that across the world there is thought to be only ONE piece of body language which is common to all people – and that is raising your eyebrows very briefly when greeting someone. Therefore, everything else is open to misinterpretation from one culture to another.

This means that you need to consider a few things. If you are not British and come from another ethnic group, but are likely to be interviewed by British people, in all innocence they may, misunderstand some of your non-verbal signals. Tricky. It certainly doesn't seem right that you should have to consider changing for other people. Sadly though, even trained interviewers cannot be versed in every alternative body gesture. Just to show you what I mean, here are some examples.

- In some countries it is completely normal for candidates to show interviewers photos of their families, tell them how well their children are doing at school, etc.

- Japanese women often hide a smile behind their hand, although this custom is changing.

- Some Mediterranean people are much more expressive with their hands than the British.

- American men are more likely than British men to cross their legs by putting one ankle on the other knee.

- Japanese people sometimes look at the other person's neck rather than eyes during conversation.

- In some countries, women are considered to be behaving improperly if they look men in the eye.

- In some countries, you beckon people with your hand palm up, in others with your hand palm down.

- In some countries, when you are indicating the number one, you raise your index finger, in others you raise your thumb.

- Some Muslim men consider it rude to shake hands with a woman.

So, even though it's not 'right' that you should have to consider your body language if you come from an ethnic minority, it would be unrealistic to ignore it. Misunderstandings happen even with people from the same culture, and they can affect chances of success in interview. How much more easily, therefore, might people from different cultures misunderstand each other. Also, no one (except, perhaps, Desmond Morris, who has written excellent books on the subject) can be an expert on all the varieties of non-verbal signals. If you think that any of your body language may be misinterpreted across cultures, check it out with people that you can trust. Once you have the university/college place or job you can always set about educating people.

Giving the right impression

We've already discussed the fact that the clothes that you wear say something about you, and this is indeed part of your non-verbal communication. Even if you dress from a jumble sale, you chose which clothes to spend 25p on.

The last chapter gave you a lot of tips on making a good entrance. Remember to hold your head confidently, don't look down apologetically or passively, walk with comfortable strides (not as if you're afraid of taking up much space). Generally, look as if you feel good about yourself. Sometimes interviewers agree between themselves that while one is interviewing, another will be looking at body language for any inconsistences.

Eye contact

A major factor in non-verbal communication is eye contact. If you've ever had a conversation with someone with a visual disability you may have found that the conversation did not feel comfortable, and there are good reasons for this.

Although eye contact seems so simple, in fact it's a highly complex and sophisticated set of movements allowing conversations to take place smoothly. What actually happens in a conversation is that we unconsciously pass messages to the other person about where we are in our speech by tone of voice and eye contact. Most people know these rules (often without realising it) and so know when it is their turn to speak. Here are a few points to remember.

■ In mainstream British society, it is acceptable to look people in the eye. However, too long a gaze can make the other person feel uncomfortable. (Ever seen the actor Donald Pleasance? He gives you the shivers because he doesn't blink.)

- The listener maintains more eye contact than the speaker. This eye contact, along with nods, 'mmms' and other gestures, encourages the speaker to continue. This is known as active listening.

- The speaker glances away while thinking of what to say next. This means that the speaker is looking alternately at the listener and looking elsewhere.

- Speakers who do not maintain enough eye contact can appear shifty, untrustworthy or lacking in confidence. Having said that, in some cultures, looking down is a sign of respect.

- The pupils enlarge when we are interested in something (or someone).

- Pupils get smaller when we are angry.

- To establish good rapport, you should meet the other person's gaze about 60-70% of the time.

- When you are looking at the other person, concentrate on the triangle between the eyes and mouth.

- If you want to make a point particularly strongly, concentrate on the triangle between eyes and an imaginary spot between the eyes on the forehead.

- People who blink for longer than normal periods can give a message that they feel superior to the other person or are not interested in them.

> *'I interviewed one man who failed to make eye contact with me at all. He missed all my non-verbal clues telling him he'd answered the questions enough. He rambled on and on. I eventually had to tap my pen on the table before he got the hint.'*

> ### *Quote from a college lecturer*

Activity

At a time when there would be no unfortunate comebacks, perhaps with a friend, try using non-verbal gestures which are contradictory to what you are saying. For example, try talking about something you feel very enthusiastic and positive about while using nervous body language. What happens to the discussion? Ask the other person how they felt.

Arm gestures

The way you hold your arms when you sit gives away a lot about how you are feeling. Remember, if you display one of these gestures, the skilled interviewer should take your whole body language into account, so don't worry if you suddenly become conscious of one particular aspect of your body language and start to feel awkward.

Crossed arms

This can mean "I feel cold", or, more likely in an interview situation, 'I feel defensive'. Perhaps the interviewer has made a statement or asked a question about which you feel very uncomfortable. If you see the interviewer sit back with arms folded, think back over what you have just said. Have you upset the interviewer in some way? If so, can you retrieve the situation? Perhaps you could do something like showing your palms, putting your head to one side, moving the body slightly sideways and saying, 'Well, I suppose it depends how you look at it'. (Open palms indicate honesty – try this gesture, you'll soon see what I mean.)

However, do remember to take the whole body language into account. Someone sitting with crossed arms may be feeling quite comfortable, it depends on whether the rest of their body language is attentive and at ease.

Tucking your hands under the opposite armpit

This shows that you feel superior – definitely not on during an interview.

Folded arms with the fists clenched

This shows definite hostility. Avoid doing this and watch for signs of it in the interviewer.

Using a handbag as a barrier

Women sometimes use holding a handbag as a barrier gesture – an alternative to folding arms. Do not sit with a bag on your knee during an interview, it is an even more obvious defensive gesture than folded arms.

Hands behind the head

This gesture, combined with slouching in the chair, says, 'I'm superior to you'. If this is combined with looking towards the ceiling, it effectively means that the other person can't get eye contact with you. It is sometimes used as a superiority gesture to stop the speaker being interrupted. Don't do it.

Open arms

This indicates an open approach. Open arms are when you hold them comfortably and loosely in your lap or on the sides of the chair. Open arms also make you look more approachable.

Hand gestures

No, not the rude ones! You'd be amazed at how much the hands give away. Let's look at some of the more obvious hand movements.

Thumb-twiddling

I once did a mock interview with a man who twiddled his thumbs throughout the whole 15-minute interview. He wondered why he had been unsuccessful in getting a job after five years of trying. No wonder! He was giving very clear signals. They read: 'You're a waste of space and I'm bored with the whole thing.'

Clenched hands

These can mean simply that you are sitting relaxed, but can mean also that you are feeling frustrated or tense. It all depends on whether your fingers are held loosely or gripped tight, knuckles going white.

'Steepled' fingers

Remember the game you played as a child, 'Here's the church, here's the steeple?'. This is where steepled fingers are held either fingers up or fingers down, and is combined usually with sitting back in the chair. Either way, it is often a gesture of superiority. During an interview, it is more likely that the interviewer will use it than you. Clearly, you want to look confident during an interview, but you must treat the interviewer at least as an equal. Be sure not to show that you feel superiority in any way.

The other time this gesture is used is when someone is thinking before speaking. The cluster of body language that you observe will tell you which is which (and will also tell the interviewer).

Rubbing hands together

This can be a sign of excitement. In his book *Body Language – How to read others' attitudes by their gestures* (Sheldon Press, 1995) Allan Pease points out that hands being rubbed together fast is seen as a sign that the other person will learn something to their advantage, while hands being rubbed together slowly are seen as a sign of the person being devious and dishonest. Lesson for you? If you're excited or enthusiastic about something you're talking about (as indeed you should be at some stage during the interview), make sure you don't rub your hands together slowly!

Hand-to-face and hand-to-head displays

Apart from eye contact, these are probably the most easily observed as people are generally looking at your face. And do they give away a lot!

Scratching the neck

This is usually a sign of uncertainty, and may mean that you are saying one thing while thinking another.

Hand in front of mouth

This can sometimes mean that you are lying – almost as though you half hope that the other person won't hear you properly, and won't notice the porky.

Fiddling with your collar

This is usually a sign that you are feeling uncomfortable about something (getting hot under the collar?). The skilled interviewer would notice this and probe a bit deeper into whatever you were talking about.

Rubbing the back of your neck

This can mean that you feel you are having a hard time (a bit of a pain in the neck?). You may be having difficulty thinking of a good (honest) answer, or be feeling frustrated or angry about something.

Leg movements

This is where the interviewer really needs to have the desk out of the way, or they'll certainly miss some interesting body language.

Crossed legs

Like other non-verbal signals, this should not be considered in isolation. Most people cross their legs simply to get comfortable or because they are cold. However, if crossed legs are combined with crossed arms and tense shoulders, they are likely to indicate displeasure or discomfort. In an interview situation, this is likely to make you appear unfriendly and unapproachable.

Crossing the ankles

This can indicate a defensive feeling. Again, the observant interviewer will notice this and probe deeper. However, combined with relaxed body language elsewhere, this is unlikely to be read in this way.

Fidgety feet

This can indicate impatience or boredom.

Mirroring

This is an interesting phenomenon. When two people are really getting along well, they will frequently 'mirror' each other's body language – that is, they will both perform some action at the same time. The movement may not be exactly the same, but will be very similar, for example, both people lean forward at the same time or scratch at the same time (but not necessarily the same place, and not each other!). But this is the best one – just watch next time you're in a pub or restaurant – people will take a swig from their drink at the same time. Now that you know this, you'll feel really self-conscious when you do it. But congratulate yourself, this is a sign that you are increasing your skills of observation and rapport with others.

If the skilled interviewer notices that you are looking tense, he or she should help you to relax by sitting back comfortably in the chair and trying to get you to 'mirror' their action. A poor interviewer will unconsciously mirror your tense body posture and the conversation will not flow smoothly. If your body language is positive and you happen to notice that the interviewer is mirroring you, it's a good sign.

Non-verbal leakage

No, nothing to do with incontinence aids, but certainly an aid to the observant interviewer. 'Non-verbal' leakage is a term used to describe an action that people perform when they are trying to cover up a feeling. Because most of us are fairly skilled at covering up our feelings with neutral facial expressions (this is where the expression 'poker face' comes from), it is as if the discomfort has to leak out wherever it can. This can be in a scratch, a fidget, a wriggle, a sigh, almost anything. The point is, you probably won't know that you're doing it.

In the interview situation, this will not tell the interviewer what you are trying to cover up, but will suggest that there is something about what is being discussed which needs further probing. Of course, the interviewer may be wrong - you may be thinking 'Where's the loo?' or 'Will I miss my last bus home?', but they won't know that. What they will do is reflect on what you have been discussing and ask you a more probing question.

Irritating mannerisms

One thing you definitely need to avoid is distracting the interviewer(s) with irritating mannerisms. Not many people display these, but nerves being what they are, even the calmest of us can sometimes act in unusual ways. Some examples of irritating mannerisms are scratching, twiddling with hair, fiddling with jewellery, clearing your throat, fidgeting, or saying 'um' or 'you know' a lot.

Basically, though, they are any action which is performed too frequently. If you undertake the mock interview as suggested on page 65, you should be able to check out whether you need to take any corrective action.

Activity

Next time you are in a public place watch people's body language without listening to what they are saying. What do you think is going on? Are the people friendly? excited? happy? threatening? miserable? in love? arguing? Watch for mirroring and non-verbal leakage. You'll find that you can tell quite a lot about situations without hearing a thing.

Putting it all together

I expect by now you'll be terrified to move at all! So, how does all of this knowledge help? Well, remember the mock interview. What was your body language like? Did you recognise yourself from any of the descriptions above? Is there anything that needs correcting? Do you have any irritating mannerisms that might annoy or distract the interviewer? If so, work on eliminating them. But don't, like the man in the quote, go so far as to sit on your hands throughout the whole interview – I suspect that someone had once told him that he gestures too much with his hands and he was playing safe.

In fact, my experience is that people often use less obvious body language than normal during an interview because they're almost rigid with fear. A certain amount of stillness can convey a feeling of confidence, but a catatonic state makes it difficult for the interviewer to continue the conversation. You need a happy medium.

Activity

You can start this activity straight away, without waiting for an interview date. As with any skill, you will improve with practice.

Become more aware of your body language and its effects on others. If you are having a difficult conversation with someone, try matching their body language in a general way. Don't copy them exactly, but sit forward when they do, or back when they do. Put your hands in a similar, but not identical, position. Don't worry about matching hand gestures – by the time you notice them and start moving the other person will have stopped. If you are female and matching a male don't worry about matching leg movements. This is particularly difficult if you're wearing a short skirt and copying the man would lead to embarrassment!

You will find this matching an invaluable skill for the rest of your life because it means that when difficult things are discussed, the temperature is kept low and things proceed better. Start practising this in a non-threatening situation for the first few times until you feel comfortable.

Chapter checklist

Do you:

- walk confidently into the room, shoulders back, back erect, head comfortable centred on your neck, eyes alert?

- sit comfortably, but not over confidently, during interviews? This means holding your head up, not slouching, not putting your hands behind your head.

- put your belongings down in an unhurried way?

- have appropriate eye contact?

  i)   making eye contact with all interviewers at the beginning of the interview?

  ii) giving main eye contact to the person asking the question, but glancing at other interviewers from time to time?

  iii) not looking apologetic for taking up their time?

- maintain 'open' body language? Not sitting with arms and legs folded, but looking approachable?

- avoid undue 'non-verbal leakage' of your nervousness? Scratches, fidgets, finger-tapping, etc?

- note the interviewer's non-verbal responses towards you, and act accordingly?

- take into account the differences in body language across cultures?

- smile occasionally? (very important!)

Chapter five
Sample questions and stunning answers

You should read this chapter:

- as soon as you are offered an interview either for a job or a place on a course.

By the end of this chapter you should know how to:

- anticipate the type of questions that you will be asked
- use the first few questions to help you feel comfortable during the interview
- answer 'settling-in' questions
- answer questions about your education and qualifications
- answer questions about your skills and experience
- answer questions about yourself as a person
- answer questions about your leisure interests
- answer questions about your disability, if this is an issue for you.

This chapter is for you whether you are applying for a job or a place at college or university. Although there are differences between the two types of interview, there are many more similarities. This chapter will show you how to answer questions for any of these interviews.

First of all, let's look at how you can take all the fear out of interview questions altogether and turn up really prepared. By understanding how interviewers 'design' questions you can get one step ahead of the game and anticipate what they will ask. Then, of course, you can work out how you will answer each question.

For jobs, trained interviewers will ask questions based on:

- the job description, and/or the person specification
- your application form or CV, and your knowledge of the organisation and issues currently affecting it.

For places on a course, interviewers will ask questions based on:

- your UCAS form
- your knowledge of relevant current issues
- your knowledge of the college or university
- your school/college reference.

Job applications

The trend in up-to-date organisations is to ignore the job description, asking questions instead based on the person specification. Just a reminder – a job description describes the job to be done. It is a list of the tasks undertaken by the jobholder. Sometimes you will see percentages written beside each item. In some cases this is the amount of time spent on each item, in others it relates to the importance of that item. Some employers do not make clear which is which. If you are unclear, consider phoning them before the interview and asking them. You don't want to waste time preparing thoroughly for less important questions.

A person specification describes the person who can do the job. Sometimes if you hold up the job description and person specification side by side, you can see a direct link. For example, one item on the job description might say 'Type Manager's letters and reports'. The corresponding item on the person specification might say 'Able to type at 45 wpm'.

However, a person specification will cover those less obvious personality-based items that are important to any employer. These may be things such as:

- able to work as part of a team
- able to work on own initiative
- reliable
- honest
- able to maintain confidentiality
- organised.

Many organisations mark against each item in the job description, person specification (or both) whether they are essential (E) or desirable (D).

Anticipating questions

By keeping these points in mind you can work out fairly accurately what an interviewer might ask you. Indeed, you will often realise that they could ask you two or three questions based around one item on the job description or person specification. Here is an example for a clerical job in a busy office where confidentiality is important.

Person specification item	Possible questions
Able to work under pressure	'In what situations do you feel most stressed?' 'When you have more to do in a day than you can possibly complete, what do you do?' 'How do you prioritise your work?'
Able to maintain confidentiality	'With regard to confidentiality, what do you think is important when you leave your desk unattended?' 'Why do you think confidentiality is important in this job?' 'What would you do if, during the course of your work, you found out something very confidential about a relative or friend?'

By working through possible questions in this way, you can decide how you would answer them. A good tip always is to try to think of an example that you can use to back up your answer.

Later in this chapter we'll look at some typical questions and how to answer them.

Interviews for university or college

Interviewers will base their questions around:

■ your UCAS or college application form

■ the reference from your school

■ details of the course and university or college

■ current issues relating to your proposed area of study.

As with job interviews, this means that you can work to anticipate the questions that you might be asked.

Possible questions

Here are some possible questions that are common to both job and course interviews.

Questions to test knowledge, experience and skills

■ Tell me about your work experience.

■ What exactly did you do when you were there?

■ Take me through a typical day.

■ What experience have you had at…?

Questions to test work approach and values

■ If I were to spend a week with you, what would I notice about the way you work/study?

■ What was the most valuable thing you have learned from your work experience/course?

- How do you organise your time?

- What do you do when you realise that you have done something wrong?

- How do you react if someone criticises you?

- What would you do if you found that one of your colleagues was cheating?

Questions to test decision-making, problem-solving and judgement

- What decisions are most difficult for you to make?

- If you had to make a decision that you had never made before, how would you do it?

- Why would you approach it that way?

- What alternatives would you consider?

- What would you do if you disagreed with a decision that your boss/ lecturer had made?

- How would you keep up-to-date with the issues involved in this job/course?

Questions to test relationships

- What type of people annoy you?

- Why?

- What do you do about it?

- What three good things would a friend say about you?

- What three things would your friends moan at you for?

- Describe yourself using six adjectives.

Questions to test your hopes for the future

- Where do you see yourself in five years' time?

- What career plans do you have?

- What training do you think you will need for this job?

- What will you find most difficult about this course?

Questions to test your interests

- How do you spend your time out of work/school?

- What do you like to read?

- How much time do you spend on each of the activities you mention on your application form?

Questions to test your circumstances and health

- Tell me about your health.

- How many days have you missed during the last year because of ill health?

- What do you think is a satisfactory attendance record?

Questions to test self-awareness

- Summarise your main strengths.

- Tell me three strengths and three weaknesses of yours.

- How do you motivate yourself when you're feeling flat?

- How would you get yourself out of a bad mood?

- What would you do if a colleague or your boss upset you?

Questions specific to college or university interviews

- Why do you want to come to this college/university?

- Why do you want to do this course?

- What interests you most about this course?

- What have you already read about the topic you want to study?

- What career plans do you have?

- What qualities will you bring if we offer you a place?

- What out-of-school activities do you follow?

Questions based on your application form or CV

Remember that interviewers will almost certainly ask questions based on what you have said about yourself on your UCAS form, application form or CV. Study it carefully and ask yourself what they might pick up as being of interest. Work out the questions that they might ask you and how you will answer them.

Questions relating to disability

If you are disabled it is likely that the interviewer will need to ask you questions to ensure that they are able to provide the facilities to employ you. Employers, colleges and universities have a legal duty to employ disabled people if they can do so with reasonable adaption to buildings or equipment and if the person is suitable for the job or course.

However, it is unlikely that many interviewers would understand the wide variety of disabilities and aids available and it may be that you will have to help them out here. While of course you would not be expected to give costings, it could be that you know that you need a particular piece of equipment. If so, be ready to discuss this as necessary.

Remember though that the interview is about you as a potential member of staff or student, not as a disabled person.

Activity

Look at your UCAS form, application form or CV and make a list of all the questions that you think an interviewer might ask you. Then write how you would respond to these questions.

Questions and answers

Here are some suggested answers to typical interview questions. There is rarely one right way to answer a question and your own situation will determine exactly what you say.

Remember that the interviewer wants to be convinced that you have the maturity and readiness to take on the responsibility of the job or to complete the course. They will also be looking for a positive attitude towards the organisation, university or college and at least a basic understanding of the specialist language of the field. Naturally, they will expect enthusiasm about the work or area of study and a commitment to succeed.

Settling-in questions for job and course interviews

The interviewer is likely to begin the interview with some very easy-to-answer questions. This is done so that you can relax and get your brain in gear. If the interviewer collects you from the waiting area, you may be asked the first question as you walk to the interview room. These questions may be something like:

Q: 'How was your journey?' or, 'Did you find us okay?'

What is the interviewer looking for?

The interviewer is just settling you in. You may have got on the wrong bus, were chased by a Rottweiller, but don't say so. You say something like,

A: 'Fine. I was surprised at how quickly I got here. The buses are quite convenient.'

Why:

This is a tiny plus point from a starter question. It lets the interviewer know that you are capable of finding your way around. Don't worry too much about selling yourself with this type of settling-in question though, there will be plenty of opportunity for that later.

Q: 'Tell me about yourself.' – a common question for job and course interviews

What is the interviewer looking for?

The interviewer wants to know about you in relation to the job or course. This might include information about your home life if it's relevant to stability – whether or not you'll stay in the job after the company has spent time and money training you or see the course through to the end. But this is not the time to tell the interviewer that you've got a cat named Toto and your little brother is a pain in the neck.

Tell the truth but be selective, remembering that the interviewer is really interested in you in relation to the job or course.

Supposing you are looking for a job. You left school 18 months ago and have been working in a book shop. You're now applying for a job as a bank clerk. Look back at your research. What were the 'essential' features mentioned in the information that you received? What skills, knowledge and experience do you have which are relevant? You may answer something like:

A: 'Well, I'm 18 and I've lived in this area all my life and come from a close family. I enjoyed school and did well with my exams. When I was looking at careers options, I realised that I enjoyed being with people as well, so I took a job in a bookshop so I could combine two interests. But now I've realised that I'd like a job which offers more challenge and has more career prospects. My family have been with this bank for years and it has a good reputation. That's why I've applied for this job now.'

Why:

This answer gives an overview of relevant information about yourself in relation to the job.

Q: 'Do you feel confident that you know all about the job you're applying for?' or 'Have you had a chance to study the course details?'

What is the interviewer looking for?

This question may follow on from the interviewer telling you about the job or course at the beginning of the interview. Alternatively, it may be a settling-in question. Let's assume that you have a pretty good idea, but however good job or course descriptions may be, you will probably think of some area where you are not clear. They may be from your prepared list of questions to ask at the end of the interview.

A: 'Well, I got a lot of information about the job/course from the material you sent me, and I'm really interested in ... One thing I'm not clear about though, what proportion of time is spent on each area?'

Why:

This shows that you've really studied the job or course description and are interested in further details. It might give you an opportunity to sell yourself further. For example, if the interviewer says 'about 20% of the time is spent speaking to customers on the phone', you may be able to reply that you enjoy telephone work.

Activity

Imagine that you have just been invited to 'tell a prospective interviewer about yourself'. Keep in mind the job or course that you are applying for. What would you say? Make some notes and keep them in your interview file.

Education questions

While education questions may not feature much in interviews as you get older, they are likely to be quite important at this stage of your life, whether you are applying for a job or a college place. Typical education questions include the following:

- When did you leave school?

- What school did you attend?

- What qualifications did you get?

- What was your favourite subject at school?

- What subject did you dislike most?

- Did you play sports?

- What do you think school or college really taught you?

- What did you enjoy most about school or college?

- What did you like least about school or college?

- What did you do to prepare for this interview?

- Did you belong to any clubs outside school?

- What work-shadowing did you undertake? What did you learn from it?

- Why did (didn't) you go on to further education?

- Would you like to continue your education in any way? How?

- Did you take any extra responsibility at school, such as being a prefect?

- What did you do in your year off?

Let's look at some of these in detail, then you can try to answer some for yourself.

Q: 'What did you do to prepare for this interview?'

What is the interviewer looking for?

To see if you have used enough initiative to prepare properly for the interview.

A: 'I read up about the university/college/organisaton on the internet and managed to speak to someone who knows this course/organisation. I tried to anticipate the questions you might ask. I also made sure I knew where to come, times of buses, etc.'

Why:

You've shown that you have real initiative. Any interviewer would be impressed by an answer of this type.

Q: 'I see you are taking three 'A' levels. How many hours a week do you study at home?'

What the interviewer wants to know:

Here the interviewer want to know that you are prepared to put in the time necessary to pass your courses, and whether you are struggling just to keep up at your current course level. If this is the case, it could indicate that you might not be able to keep up with a more demanding course or job.

A: 'I usually spend about an hour and a half each evening studying, and take advantage of any spare periods during the college day. I study for about five hours over the weekend as well. I think that having a social life is important though, so I always give myself Friday evenings off and go out over the weekend at some time. I think the important thing is to plan ahead to get the work done, but be flexible if necessary.'

Why:

This shows that you are able to plan ahead, manage your time effectively and yet still have a social life. It also demonstrates that you are that desirable creature – a rounded person.

> *'We always get a reference from the headteacher and we really take notice of what they say. For example, if a student did less well in an exam because of teacher illness, we take that into account.'*

Quote from a university lecturer

Activity

Make some notes on your answers to the questions below on a sheet of paper. Remember, if you go for more than one interview, you will need to review these answers to fit in with the job/course requirements. Keep your completed sheets in your interview file.

Q. What work-shadowing did you do at school? What did you learn from it?

How will you answer the question?

What strengths will you highlight?

Q. *What was/is your favourite subject?*

How will you answer the question?

What strengths will you highlight?

Self-awareness questions

As we have seen already, these questions are often asked at interview. They are not of the 'How many girlfriends have you had?' variety, but are personal in as much as the answers that you give demonstrate the sort of person you are, as opposed to your skills and education. Often these questions can be the most tricky because the interviewer's aim is to get you to reflect on yourself as a whole person. In addition to the list already provided you might be asked:

■ Why do you want to do this job or course?

■ Why should we offer you the job/place on the course?

■ What are your strengths/weaknesses?

■ Where do you see yourself in five/ten years?

■ How did you get on with your boss/teacher?

■ Why do you want to come here?

■ What have you achieved in life so far?

■ What do you think your references will say?

■ What do you think you can offer this organisation/course?

■ Tell me about something you have done which you are proud of.

■ What do you think is the most important thing about being a ...?

They all need a bit of thinking about, don't they? Let's look at a couple of the more common ones.

Q: 'If people were talking about you, what weaknesses would they feel you had?'

A: 'It's hard to know how others see you, but I suppose one weakness I'm aware of is that I can feel very enthusiastic about starting something and then get bored when it's underway. I've worked out how to overcome that though by careful planning and giving myself deadlines.'

Why:

Always answer this type of question by (a) stating the weakness; and (b) explaining how you've overcome it. Okay, so you can't spell, are moody and hopelessly disorganised. Don't say so! NEVER tell the interviewer about a weakness which you still need to work on. ALWAYS tell them about one you've cracked. You're not telling a lie, you're just choosing which bit of the truth to tell. They can always ask you for more information.

Q: 'What do you think your references would say about you?'

What the interviewer wants to know:

This is very similar to the question above, but gives you an opportunity to talk about your strengths as well as (or instead of) your weaknesses. Be realistic when you choose what to say, because the interviewer may compare your answer with the references! It's very strange, but most people would much rather tell you their failings than their good points. But, this is no time for false modesty. If you're good at something, why shouldn't you say so? Don't be afraid to sell yourself, this is a very good opportunity for you to do so.

A: 'I know that Mrs Jones was very pleased with my exam results and I imagine she would comment on that. Also, I'm very organised and like to plan ahead – I always get my work done in good time. She might say too, that although I can work alone I do like to be with other people. I was part of the debating society at school and enjoy team sports.'

Why:

With this answer you've highlighted an awareness of what one teacher thinks of an aspect of your ability and your self- and time-management skills. Also you've shown your ability to get along with other people and the fact that you like to be part of a team. Very importantly, you've talked about your ability to work alone. Five strong points in one short answer. Not bad!

> *'I asked one man the usual question, "Why should I give you this job rather than the other candidates?" He replied, 'Because I've applied for 108 jobs and this is the first interview I've had.' Sad. Needless to say, he didn't get the job.'*

Quote from an office manager

Q: 'Why should we offer you this job/place on this course?'

What is the interviewer looking for?

The interviewer wants to know that you have some knowledge of the organisation, course, university or college. THIS IS IMPORTANT so find out. He or she also wants to know that you have considered both what the organisation or college/university can do for you and what you can do for them. It is a wonderful opportunity to explain in detail all the benefits they can expect if they take you on.

A: 'Well, as you can see from my examination results, I've been interested in science for several years now. As part of my A levels, I had to do a project on environmental issues and I became very interested in this area, in fact I got a grade A for the project. I realised that I would like to have a career in this area and your company has a good reputation. I'm hardworking and enthusiastic and I learn quickly.'

Why:

You have told the interviewer that you did well throughout your A level course, not just in the exam; you are prepared to work hard; that you are ambitious and are looking ahead.

Many of the 'personal' questions are focused around these types of answer, so you need to analyse yourself as thoroughly as you can prior to the interview. Ask friends and relations how they see you too – you might get some surprises!

Q: *'What do you think you would find most difficult about being a ...?'*

What is the interviewer looking for?

A real understanding of the job in question. While the question asks about you, this might be a good time to bring in any topical issues that have been in the press or trade or professional journals.

A: (Let's assume the question was 'What do you think you would find most difficult about being a social worker?')

'I think that social work is a difficult and demanding job. You have to keep up-to-date with the legal side of things. I don't think I'd have any trouble with that. Probably I'd have most difficulty working with people who abuse their children. I don't suppose anybody likes that much. But it's an important bit of the job and if you can get the family back together again, with everyone happy, it would be very rewarding.'

Why:

You've told the interviewer that you understand that there are legal constraints on how the job is done; also that you are not unrealistic about working with difficult people, but think you can handle it and perhaps even find some job satisfaction.

(By the way, social work lecturers hate being told, 'I want to be a social worker because I want to help people'.)

Activity

Answer the questions below and keep your answers safely in your interview file.

1. Note down three weaknesses you would be willing to own up to at interview.

2. Now note how you have overcome each of these weaknesses.

3. Now make notes about three of your strengths.

4. Make notes about why you have chosen that particular course or job.

5. Make notes about why you should be given a place on the course or be offered the job.

Leisure questions

Some interviewers will consider leisure activities to be important, while others will ignore them. In your interview preparation, however, you must assume that they will study them carefully.

Some typical leisure questions are:

- What leisure activities do you enjoy?

- I see you're a member of ... Tell me about it.

- All your leisure activities are very sociable. This job involves a lot of working alone. How will you cope?

- What do you get out of ...?

- What is there about your leisure activities which would help you in this job?

- Would you describe yourself as sociable?

Let's look at a couple of examples:

Q: 'What leisure activities do you enjoy?'

What is the interviewer looking for?

The interviewer may be checking that you mention some activities that match what you say in the rest of your application form. They could also be checking that you are the type of person who would fit in with the existing work group.

A: 'I enjoy several different activities. I like to read – all sorts of books, but particularly thrillers. And I always try to get a part in the school play because I really like acting, although I'm happy to do behind the scenes stuff if necessary. Also, I like socialising – I go out a couple of nights a week with friends.'

Why:

If you can give this type of answer, you have provided information about yourself which is not dissimilar to that in earlier questions and answers. You've demonstrated that you enjoy at least one solitary activity (reading), and you've shown that you are sociable and like to be part of a team (acting), but that you don't mind doing less glamorous work to ensure that the task gets done.

> *'I always look at their interests section first. This is a very practical job. If they say they do DIY or something else practical, I feel more ready to believe that they will be able to cope.'*

> ### *Quote from a manager interviewing for a laboratory technician's job*

If you are reading this book ahead of your interview date and you really do have very few leisure activities, are there any you can consider taking up quickly? It is now that you will appreciate why your teachers have always told you to join something!

Skills and experience questions

These questions are very relevant if you are applying for a job, although you may be asked them if you are applying for some sort of vocational training.

Typical skills and experience questions might be:

- What experience do you have at ...?
- If you were faced with this ... situation, how would you handle it?
- What skills do you have at ...?

- How fast can you ...?

- How would you ...?

- What equipment are you familiar with?

- Have you ever used a ...?

- How long have you ...?

- When would you ...?

- What are the main tasks of a ...?

Let's look at some in more detail.

Q: 'What experience do you have at ... (e.g. mending cars)?'

What is the interviewer looking for?

The interviewer is trying to check your skills.

A: 'Well, I got interested in cars when I used to help my mum fix our old banger. Then I discovered that our local youth club had a car mechanics course so I joined that. I learned a lot from them. We actually stripped an engine and put it back together. I really like this type of work.'

Why:

This type of answer provides information about you and your experience. It shows that you get on well with your mother (they may think that is important when you have to work with older people). It also shows that you had the initiative to join a mechanics course and that you're a positive person – enjoyed it – and you seem to really like this type of work.

Q: 'If you were asked to write or organise a major project, how would you go about it?'

What is the interviewer looking for?

The interviewer will want to check your project and time management skills. They may also be interested in whether you involved other people or worked alone.

A: 'Well, it would depend on what the project was. I like to be organised and break big tasks down into smaller sections so that I can give myself a series of deadlines. That way everything becomes more manageable. If it were appropriate, I would also try to consult or work with other people. I like being part of a team, and teams can often achieve very good results.'

Why:

You've given a lot of information in a question like this, which could be asked at a college or job interview. You've told the interviewer that you're organised and a good time manager. You've mentioned also that you're a good 'team player' and appreciate that others have contributions to make. Finally, you've made it clear that you are self-motivated.

Q: 'What would you do if you were faced with ... situation?'

What is the interviewer looking for?

This is a hypothetical question. While the interviewer may be looking for specific knowledge or skills, if he or she knows that you don't have the relevant experience he or she'll be looking for an ability to put past experience of a similar, if not identical, nature to good use, as well as an ability to think on your feet. Naturally, all interviewers are looking for common sense and an ability to keep calm in any candidate.

A: Your answer will depend on the situation that is put to you. Remember the advice that was given a few pages back. If you have no relevant experience, KEEP CALM. Think of a similar situation and how you handled that. Just say to the interviewer, 'I haven't had to handle that precise situation, but perhaps I could tell you about a time when ...'. This is what the interviewer will want to know. It's worth repeating that you need to consider your transferable skills and experience.

Activity

Try to think of a typical situation that you might be faced with on a course or a job that you're considering. How would you answer a question about that situation so that you can bring out your strengths?

Chapter checklist

For jobs, study the job description, person specification and your application form or CV. For university or college applications, study the course details, information about the college or university and your college application or UCAS form.

- Anticipate any questions that the interviewer might ask you.

- Prepare answers, remembering to think about examples to back up what you are saying.

To help you to do this, analyse:

- any skills gained through work-shadowing, paid employment, and life experience

- how your education will help you with whatever you are applying to do

- how to present your experience in the most favourable light.

Decide how to demonstrate:

- that your analysis of yourself is accurate and positive

- that you have the strengths to do the course or job

- that you have no major weaknesses (while still being truthful)

- that you are a self-motivated and enthusiastic person.

Remember, preparation is key. Work out every question that you could be asked and how you would answer each one. Relate your answers not only to yourself and what you have to offer but also to the course outline or job description. Avoid sounding over-rehearsed, although usually this is not difficult because the same question can be asked in a number of different ways.

Chapter six
Awkward questions, brilliant answers

(and what to ask at the end of the interview)

You should read this chapter:

■ as soon as you begin to apply for jobs.

By the end of this chapter you should know:

■ how to answer difficult questions about the areas you would rather avoid

■ the types of questions you can ask at the end of the interview.

Questions you don't want to be asked

I have talked in this book about always looking at your strong points and thinking positive. Now it's cringe time. I want you to think of all those questions you really, seriously, don't want to be asked. For example:

■ Why you got sacked from your last job?

■ Why you had 20 spelling mistakes on your application form when you're applying for a job as a proofreader?

■ Why you got such poor grades?

- Why you show nothing in your 'Interests' section?

- Why you're applying for this arts course when all your A levels are in science subjects?

- Why you didn't finish that course?

- Why your form shows a year missing?

- Why you've had five part-time jobs in the last six months?

Now is the time to get out from behind the sofa and think about how you can turn these negative questions into positive answers. Remember, a good salesperson always sees an objection as an opportunity!

So let's look at some of those difficult questions and work out how to turn them to your advantage. If the questions are awkward because you are unreliable, lazy or in some other way lacking in the required skills to make you desirable to an interviewer, it's time to get working on yourself. Self-improvement is enormously satisfying. Not only will others look at you differently, but you'll soon start to feel great about yourself.

Q: 'I see that you were a member of a heavy metal band for a year. What use do you think that might be to this organisation?'

What does the interviewer want to know?

Let's assume that the interviewer isn't being sarcastic and really wants to know. We can learn something from almost every experience in life, even those which don't seem to be directly relevant.

A: 'Yes, that was a good year which I really enjoyed, even though it was very hard work. I learned a lot from it. The band had to really pull together as a team to get through a long list of gigs and always give a good performance to the audience. I learned to keep calm when everyone around me was rushing around. Oh yes, and I learned to keep my temper when I was really tired and under pressure. Not only that, I learned the business side of the music industry, negotiating prices, drawing up contracts, sticking to schedules and a whole lot more. I gained a lot of valuable experience.'

Why:

You've shown the interviewer that you can work as part of a team, that you are responsible and that you consider other people. You've also demonstrated that you are hardworking, reliable, don't panic easily and that you have some business experience. These are all very desirable qualities to any employer or university lecturer.

Remember that many skills are transferable. This means that even though you have gained them in one situation, you can use them in another. For example, you may have learned the basic principles of money management from having to make your pocket money and Saturday earnings last all week. While you may learn much more sophisticated techniques in many jobs and courses, this basic skill would be considered valuable.

Q: 'Why were you sacked from your last job?'

What does the interviewer want to know?

Basically, what's wrong with you! You may think you were sacked unfairly and this may be the case, but one of the rules of the interview game is that you don't run down ex-bosses (or teachers, or examining boards) to an interviewer. Think through why you were sacked. Was it through some behaviour which you have now changed, e.g. unpunctuality? Was it due to lack of skills which you have now gained or are willing to learn?

A: 'I had only just left school when I took that job and unfortunately my parents were getting divorced and we had to move house. I had so much to cope with that I'm afraid I became rather unreliable at work and they didn't keep me on after my three months' probation period. But, things have settled down now and I'm back to my old self. You can see from my school references that I'm usually a very reliable person.'

Why:

You have told the interviewer that you accept responsibility for the difficulties, rather than blaming other people (a very important point). You've also mentioned that you were working under exceptionally difficult circumstances, that you are now working well and can prove it.

Q: 'Why have you left the 'interests' section of your application form blank?'

What is the interviewer trying to find out?

Whether you have simply omitted to complete this section (this might show sloppiness), or whether you really do have no interests.

A: 'To be honest, I couldn't think of any when I completed the form. I realise now that I thought I had to put down extra special activities. I do have several interests though. I love computers, especially computer games, although I've taught myself how to word process and can even do some simple desktop publishing. Also, I enjoy seeing friends and go out at least one night a week.'

Why:

It really is unlikely that you have no interests at all. Do you read? What sort of books? Do you enjoy going out with friends? Where? How often? Do you enjoy handicrafts? What sort? What skills have you developed? Do you enjoy music? What sort? Do you go to concerts? With other people? Do you watch any particular kinds of television programmes, such as wildlife programmes or documentaries, that you could talk about?

Q: 'I can't see anything in your form for last year. What were you doing then?'

What is the interviewer trying to find out?

Simply, why there is a gap in your application form. Remember: if there is a gap, the interviewer has no way of knowing whether you've just forgotten to put something in, were at home having a baby, were unemployed, travelling, in prison, whatever.

A: 'Well, I tried to find a job as a secretary. I didn't have much luck. I've got a PC at home so I did practise my skills and can type 50 words per minute now. Also, I did some typing for a charity my aunt is involved in. I've realised now though, that I need more qualifications and that's why I'm applying for this course.'

Why:

You haven't emphasised the fact that you were out of work, although of course this is implied. However, you have shown that you were motivated enough to practise and improve your typing skills. You have also mentioned that you were willing to use those skills for the charity (good experience which you can talk about) and that you have considered your future and are acting responsibly by applying for further training.

Activity

On a sheet of paper, write a list of the questions that you don't want to be asked and note how you would answer them. Keep the sheet in your interview file.

Your question time

At the end of the interview it is usual for the interviewer to ask, 'Are there any questions you'd like to ask?' This is the undoing of many people because they sit there with nothing prepared. Not you though – here are some questions to make you look professional and give you a clearer idea of what the job, organisation or college are like.

Do prepare several sensible, well thought-out questions. A lecturer at a higher education college tells me that often she is asked, 'Is there much writing or reading on this course?' Well, naturally there is on any higher education course! Another irritating question is, 'How many hours a week will I have to work at home?' This shows lack of commitment to the course right from the start.

Do not ask whether the buses will get you to the college or university on time (and I promise you I'm not joking, a lot of interviewees seem more interested in this than in the course). You are an adult – find out about the buses yourself.

If it's a job that you're being interviewed for, it's bad form to ask about pay, car loans, holidays, etc at this point. (In fact, you usually are given information about pay and holiday entitlement before the interview stage.) It is okay to ask about pensions though (yes, you will get old one day!). In fact, if you haven't got the information already, you can ask the other questions when they phone to offer you the job – you'll be bargaining from a position of strength then.

> *'They asked me what my biggest weakness was and I said, "Chocolate!". It got a laugh and I got the job, but I don't know that I'd recommend this type of answer to everyone!'*

Quote from a salesperson following an interview

Here are some typical end-of-interview questions that won't be frowned on or make you look mercenary:

- When can I expect to hear if I've got the job/place?

- Who would my line manager be?

- What training will I be offered?

- How will my success be measured?

- What career/research opportunities might arise in the future?

- Can you tell me more about this ... aspect of the course/job?

- What percentage of time is spent on ...?

- Are there any new developments likely in the organisation of the company/university/college?

- What induction package do you have for new staff?

Questions specifically for university or college interviews include:

- What options are available with this programme?

- How easy is it to change programme?

- What is the drop-out rate like?

- What percentage of students get a first or 2:1?

- How did this department do in the national review of research quality in universities?

- Where will I live?

- How much is the accommodation?

- What are the sports facilities like?

- What is the social life like?

- Is industrial sponsorship available?

A few other questions you might like to consider, if you feel confident about handling them, are:

'Do you have any hesitation about my application?'

This gives you an opportunity to check whether you've given the right information about yourself and allows you to fill in any gaps. If the interviewer mentions qualities that you haven't discussed yet, you have a last opportunity to sell yourself.

'What problems do you think you may have with ....?'

Only ask this if you can reasonably anticipate what the answers might be. That way, you can make suggestions and you'll impress the interviewer no end. If you're taken by surprise, you may need to make a more non-committal answer, such as 'That's interesting' and hope they don't press you too hard for suggestions.

'Do you have any other questions regarding my suitability for the post?'

Again, this gives you a chance to provide any further information in support of your application.

'This course is just what I'm looking for. Can I tell you anything else to support my application?'

If you are applying for a job and can afford to be choosy rather than taking any job that is offered, you may want to ask more probing questions than this.

To help you remember your questions, write them down on a piece of A4 paper and put them in a plastic folder. When asked if you have any questions, take out the list even if you think that they've answered everything. There are two reasons for this. Firstly, you may have forgotten a question and will be glad to find it there on your list. Secondly, you can write some prompts for yourself on the same piece of paper. These prompts relate to points you want to make sure that you've covered at interview. Just write key words in big letters to remind yourself. The end of the interview is a good time to tell the interviewers anything that you may have forgotten earlier.

Should the interviewer have covered every question you had thought of, it's perfectly acceptable to say, 'Well, I had a number of questions when I arrived, but you've covered all of them, I don't think there's anything else. Thank you.' BUT, there's one last question you should always ask and that is: will he or she give you the place/job? This feels awkward for most people and you shouldn't ask outright, but if you word it as: 'Am I the sort of person you are looking for?', the interviewer may give you a yes or no. Or, if you're lucky (depending on how you look at it), they may say something along the lines of, 'Well, we were looking for someone with more experience of ...'. This gives you an opportunity to sell yourself further by overcoming any gaps in your apparent suitability.

Activity

On a separate sheet of paper, make a list of questions that you can ask at the interview. Remember to consider what you have learned about the company, university or college from your research. The interviewer will be impressed if it is clear that you have bothered to do your homework.

Chapter checklist

Many people face difficult questions because our lives do not always go exactly to plan. You may have to answer awkward questions about:

- poor attendance records

- ill-health

- a gap in your application

- poor qualifications

- a bad work record

or any number of other things. Be honest and admit to problems that are of your making but show that you have put them right already or are working to do so. If this is not the case, begin now.

- have you prepared a list of questions to take to the interview? These can be about:

  - further details of course/supervisors/career openings

  - facilities for students

  - pensions

  - line management/supervisor

  - when you will hear the result of your interview.

- Remember to take a smartly written list of questions with you into the interview – a scruffy bit of paper won't do.

- Be confident about saying so if the interviewer has answered all your questions already, but let him or her know that you had some prepared.

Chapter seven
Tests for selection

You should read this chapter:

■ two or three days prior to the interview (if you have reason to believe that you may face intelligence tests at the interview, you may wish to read that section of the chapter earlier).

By the end of this chapter you should know:

■ the range of tests that you may face during an interview

■ what preparation is possible prior to testing.

School again

You probably thought when you left school or college, 'Thank goodness, I'll never have to take another test!' Well, tests are becoming an increasing part of everyday staff (and sometimes university or college) selection procedures. They provide the interviewer with another piece of the jigsaw puzzle that makes up a picture of you and your abilities. The tests are intended to provide a reliable and objective way of measuring certain aspects of you as a person, or your skills. This means that the interviewer can make a more balanced judgement than based on interview alone.

While some tests are well thought-out, others can be less than objective and have some disadvantages.

Some tests are administered under a scheme called 'assessment centres'. If you are invited to an assessment centre, I recommend that you read Chapter one *Types of interviews* in conjunction with this.

Here are some other tests that you might encounter.

Skills tests

These have been around for a very long time. You want a job as a typist and they sit you in front of a PC to see how fast and accurate you are. In this way, the prospective employer can check out your skills without great trouble or expense.

Other skills which might be tested are:

- shorthand
- letter writing
- driving
- machine-stitching
- teaching
- presenting
- spelling
- map-reading

and many more.

So, if you're applying for a job which involves any of these, get practising!

Aptitude tests

There are six major aptitudes measured by these tests:

- clerical
- manual dexterity
- verbal
- numerical
- spatial
- mechanical.

This means that, for example, to test your numerical skills, you may face questions designed to assess your ability to deal with numerical data and to test your arithmetical skills. For verbal skills, you may face a list of words and be asked to identify their meaning. For manual dexterity, you will be given a task which tests your ability to do fine work (e.g. soldering, watch repair, etc). For clerical work you may be given a list of sentences which are written wrong to sort out (get this one?).

> *'I was stunned when I was given a pile of newspapers and told to construct a tower. I didn't know where to start.'*

> **Quote from a prospective student for an occupational therapy course**

Intelligence tests

Intelligence tests have received a lot of criticism over the years. There is always a debate about what intelligence is in the first place. Is it the ability to pass exams? Common sense? Also, some have been found to favour white, middle-class people. Nonetheless, they are used occasionally. If you think that you might face one, you can practise with a book called *'Succeed at IQ Tests'* by Gilles Azzopardi (Foulsham). There are also some tests that you can do free of charge on the internet.

Having said that, if you can get better scores with practice, do the tests really test intelligence or our ability to do intelligence tests? Actually, most people seem to enjoy these tests, even if they can't always get the answers. They are often similar to those found in quiz books and certainly similar to those advertisements in magazines for Mensa, the organisation for people with high IQs.

Some of these questions are along the lines of:

What's next in this sequence? A, B, D, G, ?

Insert one word that completes the words either side. PEND (. . .) HILL

Some are little diagrams or pictures in a sequence. You have to draw the next one or find the odd one out.

Psychometric tests

These tests examine aspects of personality. However, that's easier said than done, because personality is so difficult to define (there are over 17,000 words in the English language that are associated with personality). In fact, the tests are looking really at traits, rather than making a judgement about your whole personality.

Some people feel threatened by these tests, because they think that the tester will be looking into their innermost soul. What the tester is looking for, remember, are your personality traits in relation to the job or college course. Even then, what they find is only true for you at the time you take the test. We all develop with age and experience, and if you were to take the test again five years later the results may be quite different. Remember too, there is no right or wrong answer to these tests, so it's a bit unfair to call them tests at all.

Psychometric tests check out your traits in relation to a whole host of areas, including whether you are:

- reserved
- mentally active
- shy
- trusting
- conservative
- relaxed
- stable
- confident
- reflective
- impulsive
- obsessive
- outgoing
- humorous
- venturesome
- suspicious
- happy to experiment
- tense
- autonomous
- happy
- risk-taking
- expressive
- susceptible to guilt.

Tests of this type usually involve answering a lot of questions in a short time, and they are usually multiple choice. They are not just the sort of questions that you used to get at school, but also questions like:

Would you rather be

> *(a) an engineer or (b) an artist?*

Do you like excitement

> *(a) a lot (b) in between (c) not at all?*

When I am in a big group, I like to take my share of the limelight.

> *(a) yes (b) in between (c) no*

If you are asked to do this sort of test, you won't have much time to think about the answers, and this is deliberate. Some tests have 'lie' questions that show whether you are trying (consciously or unconsciously) to make yourself look better or worse than you really are. Also, they tend to ask the same question in several different ways. So unless you've a brilliant memory for something you answered 30 questions ago and can work out that the test is trying to get the same information out of you and you can do this all mega-quick, it's not worth trying to make up your response.

In fact, if you believe that these tests have something to offer, it pays to be honest, because the tester and interviewer will know the type of person they need to do the job. If you don't fit the bill either you'll be unhappy in the job or will not do it well.

A lot of people think these tests are dodgy, and that some can be weighted to favour people with a certain background. However, many are well thought through and can be very accurate indeed. Nonetheless, they only provide one part of the selection process and very few organisations would rely on tests alone to choose between different applicants for a job or college place.

Team role tests

One of my favourite tests in this category is the Belbin Team Role Questionnaire which tests the type of role that we take in a team. It shows, for example, whether we are good at fine detail, are the sort of person who comes up with bright ideas, are a coordinator, a teamworker, etc.

When these tests were first devised, organisations got it a bit wrong. They tested people who were good at a particular type of work, then they tested everyone else who wanted to do that job. If they got scores similar to those people who were working well already they got the job. Unfortunately, this led to teams of people who were too much alike. This meant that they didn't work well as a team. For example, it's no good having a team of people who all want to be the leader! Testers know now that for a team to work effectively it needs a mixture of team types. So, if they have a vacancy and they know that they don't have anyone who's good at, for example, fine detail, this is one of the things that they'll be looking for.

Of course, if the testers have any sense, they won't tell you which team type they want, so that you can't cheat on the questionnaire.

'We sometimes give people creativity tests. One of them is to see how well they can juggle with three balls.'

Quote from an assessment centre manager

Graphology tests

Graphology tests look at aspects of your personality through an examination of your handwriting. If you see in an advertisement or job application form that you should apply in your own handwriting, this may be because the forms are being sent to a graphologist. Having said that, it could be because they just want to know they'll be able to read your writing.

As with the personality tests, it is difficult to cheat at this. It's likely that a skilled graphologist would know whether you were trying to disguise your hand-writing. You could get someone else to complete the form or write the letter for you, but what purpose would this serve? Unless you know a lot about graphology yourself, you wouldn't know who to ask, even if you knew exactly what the graphologist had been asked to find. Certainly, they are not just looking for neat handwriting.

In-tray tests

These are occasionally used to test candidates' sense of priorities, logic and time management. Some varieties also test the applicant's knowledge of one or more software packages. They vary, but will usually include a number of items requiring attention – often about 20-30. You have to decide how you will deal with them.

The content of the in-tray is also likely to vary depending on the type of job for which you are applying. However, a typical in-tray will include:

- telephone messages

- policy documents

- personnel information

- memos

- letters of complaint

- data entry.

So, you might be asked to prioritise the order in which you'd tackle the work, identify issues, make decisions based on the information provided, plan actions and answer letters. In giving you this type of activity, recruiters are looking for your ability to:

- analyse situations

- see potential problems

- find effective solutions

- plan for successful implementation

- prioritise

- consider the implications of what you read and your decisions on the business

- negotiate

- handle situations tactfully

- use your time well

- handle paperwork efficiently

- work under pressure.

When you make decisions on in-tray items, show your reasoning. Here is an example.

In-tray exercise

Time allowed: 20 minutes

1. You are provided with blank paper, a pencil and an eraser.

2. Please use a separate sheet of paper for your response to each item and write:

a) the item number

b) how you would handle each item.

Your response might be a memo, letter or email. If you delegate an item, give clear instructions to the person on how you wish him or her to handle it.

The NEO Personality Inventory

This test measures five major aspects of personality and some traits within each area. The five areas are:

a) neuroticism

b) extraversion

c) openness

d) agreeableness

e) conscientiousness.

The Employee Adjustment Survey

This test is for people who are transferring jobs within an organisation. It tests social relationships, role requirements, organisational knowledge and interpersonal relationships in order to assess how well you are managing in each area.

The Emotional Intelligence (EI) Questionnaire

As companies realise that EI is fundamental to success in business (and life), there is an increased emphasis on this aspect of employees' behaviour. This test assesses you for:

- self-awareness

- emotional resilience

- motivation

- interpersonal sensitivity

- influence and persuasiveness

- decisiveness

- conscientiousness

- integrity.

Testing and discrimination

If you think that a test you are given discriminates against you because of your gender, cultural background or physical ability level, you can contact the following organisations for advice:

- Commission for Racial Equality

- Equal Opportunities Commission

- Disability Rights Commission.

You can find details of all these organisation at your library or on the internet. (See page 145.)

Feedback from tests

Many organisations now offer feedback after they have tested you, and this can be extremely helpful. If you are not offered feedback, you could ask for it. In fact, you are entitled under Data Protection legislation to see anything interviewers have written about you. Do so politely, don't demand. The feedback that you get will help you to form a wider picture of yourself and your abilities. It may also indicate areas where you need to do some more work. Keep the notes on it in your interview file.

Chapter checklist

There are many different types of test you may face during an interview.

These include:

- psychometric tests
- intelligence (IQ) tests
- graphology tests
- personality tests
- aptitude tests
- skills tests
- in-tray tests
- team role tests.

- Have you tried to anticipate the type of tests that you may be given? Those that test the skills required for the job are probably the easiest for which to prepare. Invest time in getting these skills up to scratch.

- You won't be able to prepare for some other tests, so there's no point worrying about them.

- Do you feel familiar enough with the range of tests to stay calm when presented with one during an interview?

- Do you know what to do if you believe a test has discriminated against you because of your ethnic origin, gender or disability?

Chapter eight
Equal opportunities issues

You should read this chapter:

■ a day or two before the interview.

By the end of this chapter you should know:

■ what is meant by direct and indirect discrimination

■ when it is legal for interviewers to discriminate

■ who to contact if you feel you have been discriminated against

■ what to consider if you feel that the interviewer is asking discriminatory questions.

It is a sad-but-true fact that discrimination is still a major factor of British life. There are laws against discrimination on the grounds of sexuality, religion, race, gender and disability. Legislation against ageism will not come into force until 2006.

However, even in the areas where there is legislation there are exceptions to the rule. The Race Relations Act 1976 states that employers can advertise for, and appoint, people of a particular race where there is a 'genuine occupational qualification' (GOQ). This means an exception. A GOQ can apply in the following situations.

■ Where the job involves participation in a dramatic performance

or other entertainment in a capacity for which a person of the racial group in question is required for reasons of authenticity. An example might be the portrayal of a well-known historical figure in a play. So, for example, it would be reasonable for casting agents for a film on Ghandi to look for someone of Indian origin.

- Where the job involves participation as an artist's or photographic model in the production of a work of art, picture or film, for which a person of the racial group in question is required for reasons of authenticity.

- Where the job involves working in a place where food or drink is provided to and consumed by members of the public or a section of the public in a particular setting for which, in that job, a person of the racial group in question is required for reasons of authenticity. A job as a waiter in a Chinese restaurant, for example, might satisfy this criterion.

- Where the jobholder provides persons of the racial group in question with personal services promoting their welfare and those services can most effectively be provided by a person of the same racial group.

The regulations concerning discrimination against one gender are similar.

The Sex Discrimination Acts 1975 and 1986 state the circumstances in which a GOQ (i.e. an exception to the law) can apply. These include for certain kinds of work in private homes, for jobs where the accommodation is single sex, where the jobs are to do with personal welfare (such as a female counsellor in a rape crisis centre), or for reasons of privacy and decency. You can find full details on: www.eoc.org.uk/eoceng/eoccs/advice/guide.asp

Yasmin's experience

'I went for an interview working in a home for elderly people. The very first question the interviewer asked me was: "Do you have any children?" I'm no expert on the law, but I do know this question has been illegal for many years.'

Discrimination as covered by the Sex Discrimination Act and Race Relations Act

So, how do you know when you've been discriminated against in relation to gender or race? Well, there are three ways in which it is illegal to discriminate against people when selecting staff:

1. in the arrangements which are made to decide who should be offered the job. This includes advertisements and instructions given to employment agencies. You do not have to be applying for the job to complain about this type of discrimination.

2. in relation to terms the of employment offered. (holidays, sick pay, etc)

3. by refusing to offer a person employment.

For both gender and racial matters, there are two types of discrimination. The first is direct discrimination. This is described by the Commission for Racial Equality in their Booklet *A Guide for Employers* as:

'treating a person, on racial grounds, less favourably than others are or would be treated in the same circumstances. Segregating a person from others on racial grounds constitutes less favourable treatment.' Direct discrimination against one gender (usually women, but it could be men) is defined in the same way.

Indirect discrimination, on the other hand is

'applying a requirement or condition which, whether intentional or not, adversely affects a considerably larger proportion of one racial group than other and cannot be justified on non-racial grounds.' (A racial group is a group defined by reference to colour, race or nationality – including citizenship – or ethnic or national origins.) Race does not include religion. Usually Jews and Sikhs are considered to be races, not religions. Again, indirect discrimination against one gender would be defined similarly.

In practical terms, this means that employers must not discriminate, for example, against married women as opposed to single women, or against women with children as opposed to childless women. Nor should there be discrimination which makes assumptions about the types of things that women or men can and can't do. This means that interviewers should not ask questions such as the following, some of which have been reported to the Equal Opportunities Commission:

- Are you engaged?

- Marital status?

- Do you live with parents/relatives, etc?

- Are your parents happily married?

- Any plans to have a baby?

- How would you feel about working in an all-white office?

- Are you on the Pill?

- How would you feel about working in an all male office?

- Do you have any period problems? (It's hard to believe that anyone would be so crass as to ask such a question, but they do.)

If you think that you have been discriminated against at work, you can take the matter to an industrial tribunal.

For any further advice on sexual discrimination contact The Equal Opportunities Commission (see contact details on page 145).

If you think you have been discriminated against because of your ethnic origin contact the Commission for Racial Equality (see contact details on page 145).

Disability Discrimination Act 1995 (DDA)

The definition of disability discrimination is not set out in the same way. However, you may have been discriminated against if you believe that:

- you were the best candidate for the job

- you could have done the job with 'reasonable adaptations' to the building or equipment.

If you believe that you have been discriminated against in this way telephone the Disability Rights Commission. The DRC Helpline provides information and advice about all aspects of the DDA and can advise on specialist organisations to contact if necessary. It also offers practical advice on employment for disabled people. Their website is www.drc-gb.org and their email address is enquiry@drc-gb.org. This site is full of useful information, including links to other sites. Also, you may like to look at the website for the Department for Work and Pensions (DWP).

Employment Equality (Religion or Belief) Regulations 2003

This act makes it illegal to discriminate against someone because of their religion. As with almost all equality acts, there are a few exceptions. For example, religious schools may advertise for teachers of the same religion.

If you think that you have been discriminated against when applying for a job or course, firstly, tell the person who has acted in this way – they may not be aware of the law. Alternatively, you can take action against the person or organisation through a tribunal or county court.

Employment Equality (Sexual Orientation) Regulations 2003

This act makes it illegal to discriminate against someone because of their sexuality. Again, there are a few exceptions. For example, someone who is a spokesperson for a gay rights organisation could be expected to be gay themselves.

If you think that you have been discriminated against when applying for a job or course you can take action through a tribunal or county court.

To complain or not to complain

Your first instinct may be, 'Oh course I'm going to complain. I'm going to nail the so and so to the floor!' If someone makes a discriminatory remark during an interview, you've every right to be outraged. **But**, consider:

- was the person being vindictively or unthinkingly prejudiced? (You may think that it doesn't matter which, but it does. Someone who's vindictively prejudiced will give you a hard time if you have to deal with them in future. Someone who just makes a silly remark may be relatively harmless, in as much as they are not out to get you or simply have not thought through the issues.)

- do you really want the job or college place?

- if you do, will you have to deal with the prejudiced person much?

- if yes, do you think you can bear it?

- if yes, do you think you can change them enough to feel that you can cope?

- if no, can you ignore the person?

- how much do you need the money?

- what risks are involved?

If you seriously want the place or job and can tolerate the person, think about not saying anything at the interview, but working on them from within the organisation.

If you don't want the place or job for any reason, challenge the person, gather your belongings and leave the interview. Even so, **don't be rude**. Act assertively – you can get your point across just as effectively. You can simply say something like: 'I find that remark offensive and discriminatory. I will stop this interview now and shall be contacting the Equal Opportunities Commission (or Commission for Racial Equality or Disability Rights Commission).'

Chapter checklist

This chapter has discussed discrimination in interviews. There are five different types of discrimination recognised by law, based on:

- race or ethnic origin

- gender

- disability

- religion

- sexuality.

You can be discriminated against directly or indirectly.

In some cases it is possible for employers to state that they need to hire people of a particular gender, race, religion, sexuality or with a particular level of ability. For matters relating to race or gender these exceptions are known as Genuine Occupational Qualifications.

People with disabilities who are best for the job should be employed if the workplace or equipment can be adapted at reasonable cost.

Do you:

- feel confident that you will know what to say if someone makes a discriminatory remark to you during an interview? Have you thought through the implications?

- know what steps to take, if you believe you have been discriminated against?

Chapter nine
The offer and reviewing your performance

You should read this chapter:

- as soon as possible after the interview.

By the end of this chapter you should know:

- how to review your performance
- what notes to make for future reference
- what to consider if you decide to write a follow-up letter
- what you need to do to update your jobsearch file
- how to respond to a job or college offer
- what information a job offer should include.

The show is over

Well, thank goodness, that's the interview over. You can relax and have a well-earned cup of coffee. But before you try to put the whole thing out of your mind until you hear the outcome, make some notes on your experience.

So you may get this job or a place on the course and not need to reflect on your experience for a while. But unless you stay in one place for the rest of your life, you will need to do so at some stage. I can tell you from experience of people on courses that often the people who are most nervous are those who haven't had an interview for years and have forgotten what to expect.

So take a few minutes now to review, it can save you a lot of time later. On a piece of paper, make notes on the following.

The journey

- Did you arrive on time?
- Did you arrive feeling calm?
- Would you have done anything differently, with hindsight?

Your body language

- Did it feel comfortable?
- Were you receiving good body language 'messages' back from the interviewers? If not, why not?
- Do you need to change any aspect of your non-verbal communication? If so, what? How will you go about it?

Your clothes

- Did they feel comfortable?
- Did they feel appropriate?

The questions

- What were they? Write down every one that you can remember. You may be asked them again in future.
- Had you worked out in advance all of the questions that you were actually asked? If not, what can you learn from the ones that you missed?
- Did you do enough research?
- Had you done enough preparation generally?

Your answers

- Were you happy with them? If not, what would you change next time?
- Were you pleased about the way you spoke?

Your questions at the end of the interview:

- Did they sound okay?
- Have you thought of anything else that you would have liked to ask?

Additional information

■ Did you need to give the interviewer any additional information at the end of the interview? If so, were you happy with the way in which you gave the information? If not, what would you do differently in future?

Your attitude

■ Did you sound enthusiastic and positive?

■ Did you let the interviewer know that you had at least a fair number of the personal and professional qualities that you identified?

Any tests, group discussions, etc

■ Were you happy about how you did? If not, what could you have done differently?

■ Have you been offered feedback? If not, will you request it?

Follow-up letter

Sometimes, it can be worth considering whether to write to the interviewer(s) immediately after the interview. There is no hard-and-fast rule about this. You will need to judge for yourself whether this will be seen in a positive light or not. While it is done occasionally, it is not common practice in this country, and you may decide to write only if you have something extra that you want to say.

Of course, it is not unusual for colleges or universities to tell you on the spot whether you have a place (or the grades that they want from you) and many employees phone candidates the same night or next day with results. However, if you have been told that there will be some delay before a decision is made, you might choose to write a brief letter. The advantages of such a letter can be that:

■ it can keep you in the mind of the interviewer(s) – a plus if there are a lot of people being interviewed

■ it provides an opportunity for you to say something that you missed during the interview itself.

So, you must decide. If you think you will write, keep the letter fairly brief and ensure that it is beautifully typed. It must sound positive and sincere. Start by thanking the interviewer for seeing you. Then let the interviewer know that you are still enthusiastic about the challenge that the job presents, and that you look forward to being able to use your skills to good effect. Use positive words like 'enthusiastic', 'enjoy', etc.

It is unlikely that many people would be irritated by a letter like this, but use your judgement when deciding whether to write one. You never know, it may be that the interviewer is having a tough time deciding between the candidates and your letter may just swing it.

There is a sample letter below.

---

2 Stone Road
Tyneford
TN7 3HG

Ms. G. Sutcliffe
Kew Manufacturers Ltd
98 West Vale Street
Tyneford
TN7 9EO

20 July 2004

Dear Ms. Sutcliffe,

re:........................... (name of vacancy)

Thank you for interviewing me today for the above post. I enjoyed meeting you and Mr Roberts.

I particularly appreciated the opportunity to look around your site and was very impressed by the work being done by your organisation. At the interview I omitted to mention that I have experience in .... and thought you might like this information. I have undertaken this work for six months during some voluntary work with a local charity and I feel sure that the Chair of the organisation, Mr J. Loor at 53 Kelsea Crescent, Tyneford TB88 7RR, would be happy to confirm this information.

I feel very enthusiastic about the possibility of joining your company, as I feel sure that my ...... and ..... skills could make a positive contribution to the .... department and its targets.

I hope to speak to you again soon.

Yours sincerely,

Yasmin Singh

Follow-up phone call

You may prefer to phone your interviewer if you have additional information to give. Here is a sample conversation:

Begin positively and considerately

'Hello, Mr Jopil, This is Yasmin Singh phoning, you may remember that you interviewed me this morning for the post of trainee manager. I realise that I forgot to give you some relevant information. Is now a good time to discuss this?'

Provide missing information

'I realise that you would probably be interested in the fact that I have stage managed three plays while at university. This involved a good deal of coordination of both people and materials as well as working within a very tight budget. I had three assistants and had to ensure that we worked together as a team. I really enjoyed doing this as I love getting the best out of people. We had a really clear goal and things went very smoothly every time.'

Thank the interviewer and ask if they'd like to know anything else

'Thank you very much for letting me explain this to you. Is there anything else I can tell you that might help to support my application?'

The job offer

How job offers are handled varies enormously. Some organisations phone people on the same day as the interview to tell them the result. Others write immediately. Still others write at a future date. Sadly, some don't get in touch at all. It is perfectly okay to ask the interviewer at the end of your interview, 'How soon can I expect to hear the result of this interview?' Generally, they will tell you both the date and the method of contact.

So, let's assume the organisation has decided to offer you that job you dreamed about. Congratulations! Soon you will be taking the next step in your career.

You probably think that this is all there is to it. But in fact, before you accept any job, you should make sure that:

- you really want the job

- you know (and are happy with) all the terms and conditions of the post.

In relation to jobs, the fact that you may get a phone call or a letter fairly soon after the interview means that you need to get your thinking cap on. Questions to ask yourself include:

- Do I really want this job?

- How do I feel about the people I met at interview? Would I feel comfortable working with them?

- Am I happy about the amount of training that I will receive?

- Am I happy with the salary that is being offered?

- Is there anything else that I need to know before making a decision?

There are also some things that you should check before you formally accept the job. A job offer should include details of the starting date, salary, place of work, hours of work, overtime arrangements (if any), holidays, pension, perks such as travel allowances (if any), sickness entitlement, job title, and job description.

You should have this information in writing before you accept the job. If you already have a job, do not give in your notice until you receive an offer in writing.

Negotiating salary

Most aspects of a job offer are part of a fixed package, but the same is not always true of salary. At the beginning of the interview some employers will say: 'We've looked at your application form and should we offer you this post we will be offering a salary of £... Would you be happy to accept that?' From the employer's point of view this makes sense – there's no point continuing the discussion if you won't accept the salary and they have no leeway.

However, for most jobs there is some leeway in salary being offered. So, what if you are not satisfied with what is offered? At this stage in your career you probably can't be pushy, but there may be some room for negotiation. Some organisations will make you a low offer in the hope that you will accept, but this doesn't mean that they are not open to negotiation.

If you think that you're worth more than is being offered, you could say something like: 'Well, I was hoping for £...' or 'Well, I was hoping for a little more.' You'd be surprised how often this works. Aim a little higher than you expect to get and then you can meet them halfway. Don't be offended if they don't budge and meet your figure. Perhaps they really don't have the money to spare, or they simply think that's all the job is worth (even if you are brilliant). You will be able to tell pretty quickly if what you have been offered is the flat rate for the job.

Finally, if your offer arrives in a letter, you have the choice of whether to phone or write in reply. If you need any further information or want to negotiate terms, then it is probably more sensible to phone. It's quicker and, from the employer's point of view, if you decide not to accept the job they can offer it to their second choice without delay.

The acceptance letter

233 Overstone Road
Cambridge
CB4 4TT
01223 555555

Mrs D. Weald, Manager
Smith's Ltd
12 High Street
Cambridge CB1 1AA

4 August 2004

Dear Mrs Weald

Receptionist vacancy

Thank you for your letter of 3 May offering me the position of receptionist at Smith's. I am very pleased to accept your offer and agree to the terms and conditions outlined in your letter.

I look forward to meeting you again at 9am on Monday 23 August.

Yours sincerely

Rachel Brown

Higher education course offers

You apply for most degree courses through UCAS, who then distributes your application form to the institutions to which you have applied. They also tell you each institution's decision on whether to offer you a place or not (usually after you have been for an interview). They generally make you one of two kinds of offer: conditional or unconditional.

Conditional offer

The conditions applying to this offer are that you pass certain exams at certain grades. This kind of offer is made when you apply prior to taking your examinations. If you meet the conditions specified when your results come out, the college or university **must** give you a place.

Unconditional offer

This will make you feel good. An unconditional offer is just that – unconditional. The college or university is happy with you just as you are, with the qualifications that you have. This type of offer is usually made to people whose exam results are known already, or occasionally to mature students prior to their results being known. You still need to tell the college or university that you are accepting the offer.

Choosing your firm and insurance offer

When you have received all the offers that the universities/colleges are going to make, you then have a choice. You must choose one offer as your 'firm' offer (or first choice) and another as an 'insurance' offer (or second choice). Your firm offer should be the institution that you really want to go to – if you make the grades for this offer, you will be given a place there automatically.

For your insurance offer it is sensible to choose a university/college that is asking for lower grades than your first choice. Then, if you don't do quite as well as expected, you may still get your second choice.

When your results come out…

If you have achieved the grades requested by your first choice, you don't have to let them know – they will have been informed.

If you make your second offer but not your first…

If this is the case for you, you will be given a place by your second choice. But if you only missed the grades that your first choice were asking for by a narrow margin, it is worth contacting them, as they may still give you a place.

If you do not make either offer…

If this happens to you, it's definitely worth phoning the institutions as soon as you have your results. Enthusing about how much you want to do their course or explaining why you missed that one grade might swing a decision in your favour. There's no harm in trying. Equally, you may be in a year where many people failed to get their expected results, so you could be lucky. But bear in mind that they may have many, many people phoning and they may need time to make decisions about people in your situation. Be patient if they ask you to wait and phone back a few days later.

If you contact the universities/colleges for any reason, remember to have your UCAS number to hand. It will save a lot of time and hassle.

What if you miss your offers and are rejected by both institutions?

If you miss both your offers and both institutions turn you down, don't despair! There are systems designed to match students without places to courses with spaces. Scan the national newspapers and other media to find out which institutions still have places and contact the ones in which you are interested direct.

You should also make use of the Clearing system operated by UCAS. If you have been applying through UCAS but do not have a place on a course at this stage, you will be sent a form automatically.

Chapter checklist

Have you made notes in your interview file on:

- every question that you were asked and how you answered them
- how you would have preferred to answer any questions that you were unhappy about
- your journey
- your interview outfit
- your body language
- what you noticed about the interviewer's body language
- questions you asked the interviewer(s)
- your brilliant parting line
- how the tests went
- have you considered the need to write a follow-up letter?
- are you clear about the difference between conditional and unconditional university and college offers, and how to respond to them?
- do you know what you should check before you formally accept a job offer?
- do you know what questions to ask yourself to check whether a job is right for you?

Further information

The definitive book of body language – how to read others' attitudes by their gestures – Allan and Barbara Pease, Orian Press, 2004.

Job Searching online for dummies – by Pam Dixon, IDG Books, 1998.

CVs and Applications – by Patricia McBride, Lifetime Careers Publishing, 2004.

Great Answers to Tough Interview Questions – by John Martin Yate, Kogan Page, 2001.

Cover letters that knock 'em dead – by John Martin Yate, Adams Media Corporation, 1997.

Naked at the Interview – Burton Jay Nadler, John Wiley & Sons Ltd, 1994.

Some websites related to jobseeking:

www.worktrain.gov.uk

www.fish4jobs.co.uk

www.dynastaff.com – full of interesting ideas to help your interview preparation

www.connexions-direct.com – provides advice for job hunters

Organisations you may find useful are:

Equal Opportunities Commission – Arndale House, Arndale Centre, Manchester, M4 3EQ. Tel: 0845 601 5901. www.eoc.org.uk Email: info@eoc.org.uk

Commission for Racial Equality – St Dunstan's House, 201-211 Borough High Street, London SE1 1GZ. Tel: 020 7939 0000. www.cre.gov.uk Email: info@cre.gov.uk

Disability Rights Commission – DRC Helpline, FREEPOST MID02164, Stratford upon Avon, CV37 9BR. Tel: 08457 622 633. Textphone: 08457 622 644. You can speak to an operator at any time between 8am and 8pm, Monday to Friday. Fax: 08457 778 878. www.drc.gov.uk

Index

O

P

Q

R

S

T

V

W

More titles in the Student Helpbook series

NEW EDITION

CVs and Applications 5th edition
Equips you with all the information you need whether applying for a
job or college place.
£10.99   1 902876 81 4

NEW EDITION

A Year Off … A Year On? 8th edition
Packed with all the information you need to make the most of your
time out between courses or jobs.
£10.99   1 902876 86 5

NEW EDITION

Jobs and Careers after A Levels
and equivalent advanced level qualifications 8th edition
Opportunities for students leaving school or college at 18.
£10.99   1 902876 93 8

Student Life: A Survival Guide 3rd edition
Invaluable advice for anyone soon to begin university or college.
£10.99   1 902876 36 9

Careers with a Science Degree 3rd edition
Compulsory reading for anyone considering studying science at
degree level.
£10.99   1 902876 66 0

Careers with an Arts Degree 3rd edition
Brimming with all the possibilities for anyone considering studying
for an arts degree.
£10.99   1 902876 65 2

For further details please contact:

*Customer services, Lifetime Careers Publishing, 7, Ascot Court, White Horse
Business Park, Trowbridge, Wiltshire BA14 0XA.
Tel: 01225 716023; Fax: 01225 716025
Email: sales@lifetime-publishing.co.uk*